PROFILES
FOR
PERFORMANCE

PROFILES
FOR
PERFORMANCE

Total Quality Methods for Reducing Cycle Time

Jack H. Fooks

Addison-Wesley Publishing Company, Inc.

Reading, Massachusetts • Menlo Park, California • New York
Don Mills, Ontario • Wokingham, England • Amsterdam
Bonn • Paris • Milan • Madrid • Sydney • Singapore • Tokyo
Seoul • Taipei • Mexico City • San Juan

The publisher offers discounts on this book when ordered in quantity for special sales.

For more information please contact:

Corporate & Professional Publishing Group
Addison-Wesley Publishing Company
One Jacob Way
Reading, Massachusetts 01867

0-201-56314-2

1 2 3 4 5 6 7 8 9 10   MU 9695949392

First Printing: December 1992

Contents

Total Quality Defined
The Mission of the Business
The Dynamics of Investment
Using Profiles to Improve Performance
Time and Radical Change

Show Your Profile
Time Drives Quality Performance

Acknowledgments

During the 1960s and early 1970s, a small group at Westinghouse Headquarters Manufacturing Department developed a method for profiling factory inventories over the cycle time of the manufacturing process, as a means of reducing the cost of ownership of inventory. Executive sponsor and supporter of this work was Douglas D. Danforth, former chairman of Westinghouse Electric Corporation.

By 1974, the team had published its methods and was working with Westinghouse factory people to reduce cycle times and thus shrink inventory investment. This pioneering group included Marty Chlystek, Frank Gue, Dwayne Rife, and Nick Sirianni.

In 1981, under the sponsorship of Paul E. Lego, now chairman and CEO of Westinghouse, a team at the Productivity and Quality Center extended these ideas to include the notion of cycle-time reduction as a driver of radical change in both the office and the factory, and developed the macro profile technique for viewing the total business from a Cost-Time perspective. A few years later, members of this group extended the methodology to include Cash-Conversion

Analysis—a means of using the Cost-Time perspective to better understand strategic business decisions. These developments led directly to the Cost-Time methodology described in this book.

All of these Cost-Time techniques have been widely employed and successfully implemented throughout Westinghouse for more than a decade. For many years they were regarded as proprietary information, held confidential to Westinghouse for competitive reasons. Now we have decided to "go public."

I had the good fortune to be involved with the Productivity and Quality Center team during the 1980s and into the 1990s, and participated in the growth and influence of this powerful business-improvement process. I shall always be grateful for the chance to be involved with such a significant development, as well as for the opportunity to see it contribute so much to Westinghouse operations around the world.

Particular credit and thanks are due the original Westinghouse Productivity and Quality Center team, including Rich Ekstrom, Jack Meess, Ed Oppedal, Bill Roth, Nick Sirianni, Bill Terzi, and Ron Thompson.

Thanks are also due to Carl Arendt, who organized and wrote down much of this material.

It has been an exhilarating journey of discovery and accomplishment. I'm really glad I had a chance to take the ride! My hope for this book is that it will introduce you, the reader, to the same excitement and potential benefits we at Westinghouse have experienced. If that happens, I will feel even richer for the experience.

Jack Fooks
Pittsburgh, Pennsylvania
February 1992

Foreword

Paul E. Lego, Chairman and CEO
Westinghouse Electric Corporation

How do you measure improvements in Total Quality Management (TQM)? How do you know if your process is getting better? How can you decide what to do to "make things work better around here?" And, perhaps most important, how can you link TQM improvement projects to expected bottom-line results?

Cost-Time Profiling is a technique Westinghouse developed in the 1970s and early 1980s. It addresses directly those questions, and more.

Of necessity, this book provides a multi-layer explanation. For example, line managers and professionals will find full details of a superior way to manage and measure process improvement. Senior managers will also find a method for linking individual improvement-project outcomes with overall financial results for the business. And TQM practitioners at any level will find a practical, useful way to take advantage of the quantum improvements possible using cycle-time reduction as a driving force.

We've used this methodology for over a decade in every part of Westing-house—from aerospace and broadcasting to X-ray diffraction and zirconium processing. The results have been phenomenal, as this book attests. We have become so enthusiastic about this Total Quality methodology that we want to share it with everyone in the U.S. who is dedicated to improving our nation's business operations and global competitiveness.

For us, Cost-Time Profiling is an essential part of continuous quality improve-ment. We use it to quantify our efforts and to analyze our operations in offices, factories, and in the field. This book sets out the full method publicly for the first time: how to use Cost-Time Profiles for performance to benefit **your** business.

A New View of Business Excellence

Total Quality is a relatively new management model for American business. It demands new ways of thinking about and managing our enterprises.

Focused on satisfying customers through continuing excellence of performance, Total Quality requires ongoing and measurable improvement in the business. New processes—such as Cost-Time Profiling—are designed to help managers identify improvement opportunities and to help employees work on designing and implementing "better ways to do it." In other words, Total Quality improvement is largely about process improvement.

We developed Cost-Time Profiling at Westinghouse Electric Corporation to identify, understand, and quantify business process improvements. The technology turned out to have many other uses, and it has become a cornerstone of our Total Quality activities. We use it

- To measure productivity and quality performance—in the office, in the factory, and in the field

- To find better ways to create value for stakeholders while reducing investment

- To quantify the linkage between results of individual improvement projects and the financial performance of the overall business

- To quantify and reduce the "invisible inventory"—the investment in knowledge and information that fuels white-collar operations

- To significantly improve investment turns

- To involve employees at all levels in improving performance productivity and quality, including effectively measuring and communicating progress

- To simplify running a corporate business on a cash-flow basis by elevating time considerations to the same level historically occupied by cost considerations

- To measure the impact of cycle-time reductions on the income statement and the balance sheet

- To provide powerful new strategic insights for making global, long-range choices

Cost-time methods have substantially changed the ways we manage our diverse portfolio of businesses within Westinghouse. The technique also helped our Commercial Nuclear Fuel Division win the first Malcolm Baldrige National Quality Award in 1988. It also supported Westinghouse divisions who were finalists in the Baldrige competition in 1989 and 1990. The Baldrige Award is presented annually by the president of the United States to American companies who have been judged to be the best in Total Quality Management.

Total Quality Defined

At Westinghouse we define Total Quality as performance leadership in meeting customer requirements by doing the right things right the first time.

First and foremost, we define Total Quality as **performance.** It's the sum of the performances of every person in the organization. Every employee must be involved in the pursuit of Total Quality, and improvement efforts will center on creating better processes—better ways to perform the job.

Total Quality is also **leadership,** which to us means being the best in the world. This goal requires continuous performance improvement to become and remain the best.

Total Quality means **meeting (or exceeding) customer requirements.** Customers determine how well the enterprise is doing. Satisfying customers—both inside and outside the organization—is the purpose of Total Quality performance.

Finally, Total Quality is **doing the right things right the first time:** determining the right things to do to satisfy our customers and creating ways to do those things error-free, every time.

The Mission of the Business

But just what are the "right things" for a business to do? What objectives should the "right things" address?

For a business—as opposed to a charitable or educational institution—the primary objective is to **increase shareholder value.** Increasing returns on the shareholders' equity not only provides for buoyant stock prices but also eases the availability of capital to finance further improvements and growth.

In terms of day-to-day operation, there are two types of value drivers that cause shareholder value to increase:

1. **Corporate financial drivers,** including capital restructuring, stock repurchase, and innovative financing techniques, among others. These activities are properly a major concern of the CEO and the chief financial officer and their staffs.

2. **Operating value drivers,** which can be addressed by the remainder of the organization. There are three:

    - Operating profit margin

    - Investment turnover

    - Revenue (sales) growth

The operating value drivers are directly affected by Total Quality efforts and can be dramatically enhanced by such processes as Cost-Time Profiling.

For Westinghouse managers, Total Quality is the strategy we use to improve margins, turnover, and sales—to improve value. Historically, most American companies have emphasized customer satisfaction, price realization, and cost reduction to increase sales and margins. The Westinghouse Cost-Time perspective adds total cycle time of the business to this list and uniquely focuses on **investment management, as an operational issue.**

The Dynamics of Investment

Operating managers have usually viewed investment as a static number—$10 million, $100 million, and so on. As a static entity, investment is difficult to manage. One good example is corporate inventories, which require extraordinary efforts to obtain reductions of even a few percentage points (and which usually leap right up again, as soon as attention turns elsewhere).

The breakthrough for Westinghouse came when we realized that investment is dynamic as well as static. Speaking dynamically, investment is **the flow of cash over the cycle time of the business process.** It can be measured as cost per unit of time over time. More importantly, it can be graphed, understood, and managed. This insight gave birth to the Cost-Time Profile (figure 1-1).

The Cost-Time Profile simply diagrams the accumulation of cash during each unit of time (days, weeks, months) across the entire business cycle—from negotiating an order and entering it, to pre-manufacturing design and information gathering processes, through manufacturing, to shipment and receivables. The cycle ends with collection of payments. This profile is a **cash-oriented** diagram; we will examine it in detail in Chapter 3.

The important idea at this point is this: **the total dynamic investment of the business is represented by the area under the macro Cost-Time Profile.**

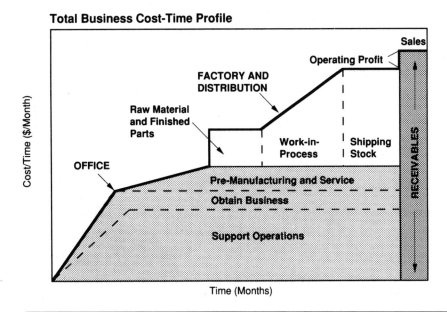

Total Business Cost-Time Profile

Figure 1-1
The Cost-Time Profile diagrams the accumulation of cash during each unit of time across the entire business cycle. The total dynamic investment of the business is represented by the area under the profile. A macro profile has three major segments: office, factory, and receivables.

To reduce dynamic investment in order to increase turnover, the key is to **shrink the total business profile** (figure 1-2). Cycle-time reduction is the principal driver for this shrinkage, aiming to reduce time by 50% or more. This approach radically lowers investment and increases operating profit margins. Reducing cycle time also tends to increase sales revenues by providing faster availability and more responsive customer service.

Note that throughout this book, the term "investment" means **dynamic investment.** The static component of investment—including property, plant, and equipment—can easily be included by simply adding its cash value to the profile cash. Dynamic investment is more directly and dramatically impacted by cycle-time reduction, lower costs of labor and material, and volume growth. Dynamic investment more directly affects the day-to-day flow of cash. Westinghouse experience is that reducing dynamic investment causes the static

Objective: Shrink the Business Profile

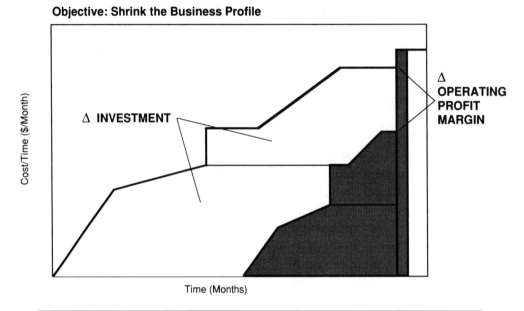

Figure 1-2
Reducing cycle time and cost—shrinking the profile—reduces dynamic investment (area under the profile) and increases operating profit margin.

investment to shrink also—one needs fewer storerooms, less factory and office space, fewer machines, and the like.

In this way, a Total Quality focus on improving individual processes has a dramatic effect on all three operating value drivers: margin, turnover, and sales. The result is a significant upsurge in business performance, customer satisfaction, and shareholder satisfaction.

Using Profiles to Improve Performance

At the operating level, Cost-Time Profiles are used for both diagnosis and prescription (figure 1-3). The total business profile is made up of individual plant and/or product-line profiles. These in turn incorporate business processes, individual operating processes, and individual sub-processes—each of which can be profiled and improved.

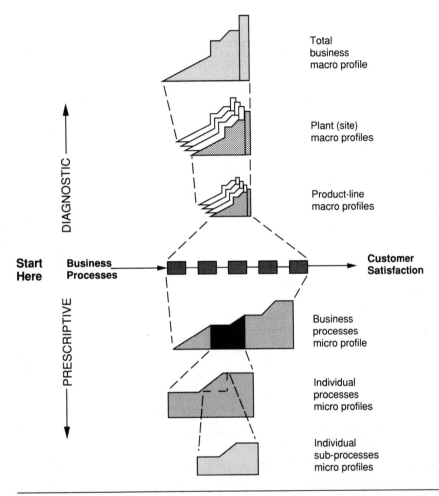

Figure 1-3
How to use Cost-Time Profiles to identify and implement business improvements.

Starting at the level of business processes, Westinghouse people in a wide variety of businesses have learned to examine Cost-Time Profiles. They determine the "right things" to do in order to improve the business and to positively affect the operating value drivers by specific day-to-day actions. Selecting the most effective improvement opportunities for the business as a whole results from examining the hierarchy of profiles to find the places where taking action and applying resources will have the greatest impact.

The results are dramatic. Widespread use of the Cost-Time Profiling method in Westinghouse was a significant contributor to the corporation's record of 29 consecutive quarters of earnings improvement between 1983 and 1990. Time-driven improvements, such as those shown in this book, are an important ongoing activity in most corporate operations. In all, Cost-Time Profiling has proven to be of tremendous value, not only in Westinghouse but also in a variety of other major companies whose people have learned, licensed, and applied the technology.

Time and Radical Change

American business has recently been awakening to the importance of time as a dimension of performance excellence. Articles in various periodicals have discussed the importance of "time-based competition"—the need to reduce cycle time of operations in addition to traditional cost-reduction activities.

Applications of this idea to date, however, have often been simply implementations of just-in-time methods. Important as they are, these techniques have not addressed cycle-time reduction in the office, where Cost-Time Profiles have a major impact. They have neither evaluated nor quantified the impact of time on the entire business, in terms of **improving the productivity of capital, enhancing operational excellence, and increasing shareholder value.** The Westinghouse Cost-Time Profiling technique affects all these vital areas in a structured, measurable, and manageable way.

As U.S. firms recover from the shock of encountering successful foreign competitors virtually for the first time, they need new models and methods to provide the improved performance that will help them to be more competitive in the global marketplace.

Cost-Time Profiling provides a proven methodology to drive the radical changes we need for business success in the 1990s and into the twenty-first century. It addresses operating areas as yet untouched by rigorous improvement efforts. And it models and measures the performance aspects of the business— the ones we must tackle to become and remain world-class Total Quality competitors.

For Westinghouse it is the Total Quality technology *par excellence*.

The Cost-Time
Perspective

We started with the perennial problem of factory inventory. During the sixties and seventies, Westinghouse people invented a variety of methods for attacking the problem of high inventories.

One of the most effective was an inventory-profiling technique developed in 1968 by Nick Sirianni, now a general consultant at the Westinghouse Productivity and Quality Center. Because he knew that turning inventory more frequently can lower the costs of ownership, he developed methods for charting cost buildups in the factory versus elapsed time of inventory possession.

A big insight followed when we realized that **time can also be a driving force for improvement.** For over a century, most companies have sought to improve performance by reducing costs. But that's only one piece of the management puzzle—the effects of **reducing time** can be even more dramatic.

We applied our time-oriented philosophy to the processes used in business—the ways work is performed—to complete the puzzle. The result, named Cost-

Time Profiling and formulated at our Productivity and Quality Center, has been in use across Westinghouse since 1982.

Show Your Profile

The Cost-Time Profiling method starts with a simple idea: any set of business activities (a process) can be defined as a collection of costs over time. The process can be as basic as machining a component or responding to a customer complaint. It can be as complex as deciding product-development and manufacturing strategies for an entire business entity.

Any process, however complicated, can be mapped and analyzed, and its cost and time dimensions charted on a Cost-Time Profile. Figure 2-1 shows a simple example.

As figure 2-2 explains, *vertical lines* on the profile represent purchased materials and services. In a factory, they're raw materials; in the office, they're supplies, outside services, and information. *Diagonal lines* represent work—dollars per hour of cost added over time. The slope of the line depends on the workers' pay rates and on the duration of the work. *Horizontal lines* are wait times—when nothing is happening to the process but time is going by. In factories, the material sits in storerooms or in the aisles; in offices, the information resides on paper in in-baskets or electronically inside computers. Reducing wait times—which can approach 95% of elapsed time—offers the most immediate opportunity for improvement efforts.

Using the process analysis and its visible result, the Cost-Time Profile, teams of managers and other employees can find ways to shrink the profile, thus reducing both the cost and the time required to perform the process.

Another advantage of using the profiles is that they clearly **communicate what's needed.** Everyone involved in a process can see what is happening. When each person clearly sees how his or her own activities affect the whole process, they then can focus on ways to implement rapid improvement.

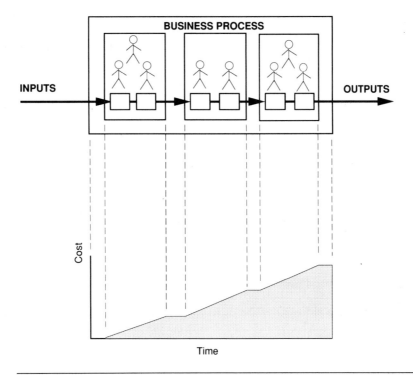

Figure 2-1

At its simplest level, Cost-Time Profiling is a way to understand business processes and identify ways to improve them. A process (top) consists of people receiving inputs, adding value, and delivering outputs. The profile (below) describes those activities in the context of the total elapsed time (or cycle time) required to perform one iteration of the process. The vertical axis represents the cost of materials, purchased services, labor, and overhead; the horizontal axis represents cycle time—total elapsed time to perform one cycle of the process.

Cost-Time Profile Components

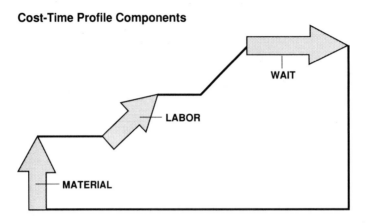

Figure 2-2
Every Cost-Time Profile, however complex, has three components. The vertical lines represent purchased materials and services, including information. The diagonal lines are labor, or work performed. The horizontal lines are wait times. Just-in-time processes in the factory, for example, are essentially techniques for eliminating the horizontal wait times from the manufacturing process.

Any process can be mapped and profiled to identify and prioritize opportunities for improving the process most effectively (chapter 4 shows how). We usually start with an objective of 50% reduction in cycle time for the process. Costs come down too, almost as a by-product of time reduction and quality improvement. As a general rule, costs diminish by some 20–30% of the percentage cycle-time reduction achieved—in other words, when we reduce a process's cycle time by 50%, we expect a corresponding 10–15% reduction in process costs.

One surprising result of performing hundreds of these micro analyses has been our discovery that actual value-added work—the diagonal portions of profile lines—generally constitutes only 10% or less of the profile's elapsed time. The other 90% is wait time—wasted time which adds no value. In our manufacturing plants, this ratio has been improving for several years as we install just-in-time methods to eliminate wait times.

And what about inventories? The area under the curve of a factory Cost-Time Profile is inventory (figure 2-3). Shrinking the profile in effect shrinks inventories. Improve the process, and the new, smaller profile measures the change.

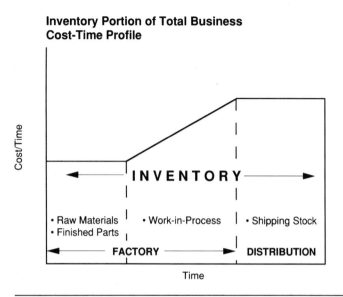

Figure 2-3

The area beneath a Cost-Time Profile (the integral of the curve) represents cash invested in the process being profiled. For a manufacturing operation, the area is inventory—either raw materials and finished parts, work-in-process, or shipping stock. Reducing inventory levels is therefore synonymous with shrinking the Cost-Time Profile of the process.

One Westinghouse division that makes electrical components for the construction industry used the Cost-Time technique to cut manufacturing cycle time by 70%, from 70 days to 21 days. Scrap, a big cost of waste, was reduced by 33%. And inventories also went down by one-third!

Between 1983 and 1991 Westinghouse permanently cut the need for inventories throughout our operations by over one-third—nearly one billion dollars—using Cost-Time methods to improve manufacturing processes and eliminate wait time.

In the office, process profiles shrink dramatically, too. But we were faced with a question: what is the area under these office-process curves, and how can we measure it? In the factory this area is called inventory; we searched for its equivalent in the office.

The problem was solved by Bill Terzi, another member of the Cost-Time development team and now a general consultant at the Westinghouse Productivity and Quality Center. Terzi observed that the profile area represents cash invested in a process. In an office, the investment is mostly for knowledge and information—commodities that are essential but not captured on the balance sheet. They're what the accountants term "period costs," the written-off costs of office and service people.

In early 1984, we decided to call this investment in office processes the "invisible inventory." It represents perhaps the biggest single improvement opportunity available to American businesses.

Figure 2-4 shows the profile for a white-collar process, the nuclear fuel reload engineering design process for a commercial power plant—a major activity of

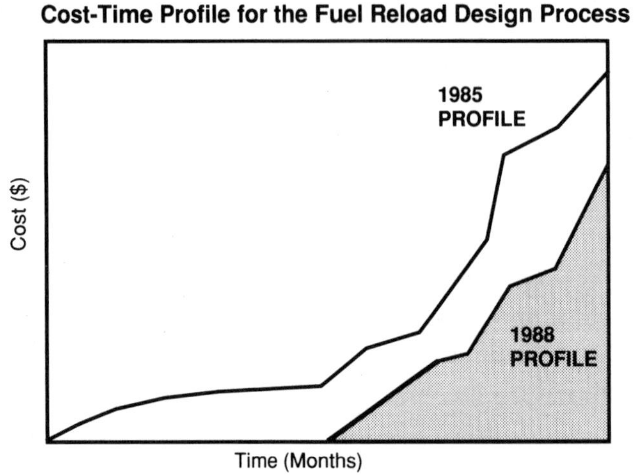

Cost-Time Profile for the Fuel Reload Design Process

Figure 2-4
Cost-Time Profiling was used at the Baldrige-Award-winning Westinghouse Commercial Nuclear Fuel Division to dramatically improve the engineering process of designing their custom product—nuclear power plant reload fuel. Through Cost-Time Analysis and many individual improvement projects, cycle time for the entire process was cut in half, with a cost savings of 21%. The engineering organization handled 40% more design activity in 1988 with only 10% more people than it had in 1985!

the Westinghouse Commercial Nuclear Fuel Division, the 1988 winner of the Malcolm Baldrige National Quality Award. This Cost-Time project cut cycle time in half and reduced costs by 21%.

The Westinghouse use of Cost-Time Profiling has revealed the importance of cycle time in driving improvements. We have demonstrated that, in the process of profile shrinking, **time is as powerful a force as the combined impact of labor and material costs.**

Time Drives Quality Performance

Improved quality performance is a major factor in shrinking the profile of a process. For this reason, Cost-Time Profiles are a vital element in the internationally recognized Westinghouse Total Quality process.

Ed Oppedal, manager of Cost-Time programs at the Westinghouse Productivity and Quality Center, believes that poor quality directly represents wasted time— time spent in waiting, in rework, in extra inspections to prevent recurrence, in fixing problems, and the like. Because a Cost-Time project challenges us to perform the process in half the elapsed cycle time or less, we can't afford bad-quality work—so quality problems get fixed as part of the project.

Oppedal points to figure 2-5 to emphasize the relationship between improving quality and reducing process cycle time. The objective in improving a process is to drive quality toward 100% and cycle time toward zero, thus shrinking the Cost-Time Profile.

But even operating that process at its maximum quality level and minimal cycle time does not represent the ultimate possible improvement. As figure 2-6 shows, you can always innovate—creatively change the process to get the result in still less time. And you can continue innovating, virtually without limit, each time producing a smaller profile with shrinking investment and dramatically improved quality and customer service.

The cycle of quality improvement and innovation becomes a continuous process—an important element of the Westinghouse Total Quality initiative.

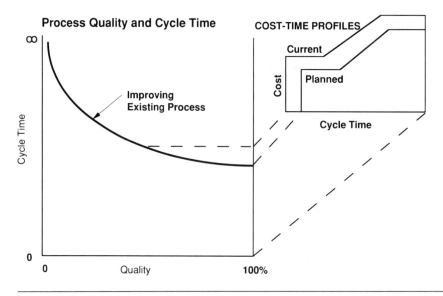

Figure 2-5
Cost-Time methods are a significant part of quality-improvement efforts. For every business process, the quality of process performance is directly related to the cycle time for the activity. Improvements in quality performance—which eliminate time-consuming rework, waits, and fixes—shorten the cycle time. Each improvement is reflected in a reduced Cost-Time Profile. At 100% quality level, the cycle time is at its minimum point for the existing process.

Looking at the Total Business Profile

By the mid-eighties, many Westinghouse units were using the Cost-Time technology to improve processes in their factories and offices. The next step was to extend the method to cover the total operations of a business.

Traditionally, we had approached financial evaluation using the income statement (figure 2-7). This **cost perspective** aggregates the total cost of sales including factory costs and office costs—managed, strategic, committed, and so on. The difference between sales billed and the total cost of sales is operating profit, the bottom line.

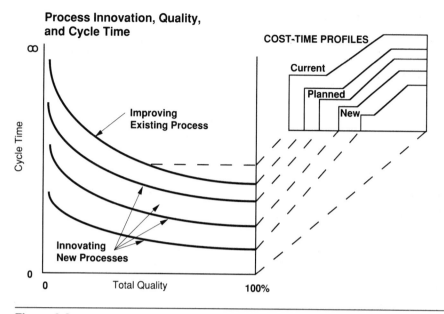

Figure 2-6
Further process improvement and cycle-time reduction come about from innovation.
Finding new and better ways to perform the work will further reduce cycle time,
shrink the Cost-Time-Profile, and provide new dimensions for quality performance
excellence. In this way, Cost-Time Profiling drives creative business-process
improvement.

Constructing a macro Cost-Time Profile of the total business (figure 2-8) adds
the dimension of **time** to that of **cost.** The macro profile provides a true view
of the cash component of the dynamic investment in the business, including the
office invisible inventory. In this Total Business Profile, the vertical axis
represents the traditional cost-oriented elements of the income statement. The
profile adds a time dimension—elements of the balance sheet—so that the area
under the curve is the shareholder dynamic investment required to operate the
total business.

This macro profile illustrates the way cash builds up over time as products or
services pass through their entire cycle in the business operation. The profile is
developed from a flow model of the total business processes—from initial
product concept through negotiations with customers to collecting receivables.

Elements of the Income Statement

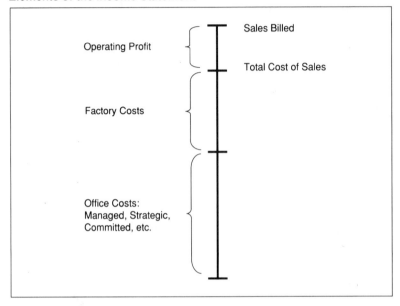

Figure 2-7
Traditional financial evaluation of a business from the cost perspective.

This point of view is usually not available to corporate executives, who have been trained to manage operating profit margins, selling price, and total cost. The macro profile, accenting cash buildup over the months of a business cycle, redirects attention to the balance sheet and opens new decision options for management. In a sense, it adds the entrepreneurial perspective of the small business owner who is focused on the amount of cash invested in the business and the time cost of that money.

The Cost-Time area in the non-manufacturing part of the profile includes processes like research and development, customer contact and negotiations, engineering drawing and specification, purchasing, manufacturing planning and scheduling, distribution, billing, and payment. These areas include the information and knowledge needed to perform all the non-manufacturing activities and services required to move from product concept to order receipt to delivery of a product or service.

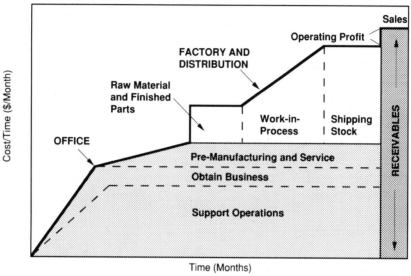

Figure 2-8

The entire business process can be described with a macro Cost-Time Profile. The profile includes factory and distribution processes involving raw material, work-in-process, and shipping stock. The profile also includes the office (white-collar) functions of research and development, negotiation and sales, as well as pre-manufacturing processes such as order entry, manufacturing information and control, and the like. The profile also includes receivables. The differential between the total cost (highest point of the factory profile) and the total sales represents operating profit for the business. A macro profile can be used to analyze and prioritize opportunities for dramatic improvement in all business operations.

This is the "invisible inventory" for the total business. We believe it presents our biggest and best opportunity to raise significantly the productivity and quality levels of American business.

Used at this macro level, the profile becomes a management decision tool. It provides a model for selecting the most effective improvement activities in terms of their overall effect on the business.

Shrinking the profile relative to sales results in higher operating profit margin and more turns of a smaller investment—true measures of performance and value creation. This kind of process improvement results in higher-quality performance and increased responsiveness to customer needs.

Figure 2-9 shows the macro profile developed by one Westinghouse division, projecting their strategic needs three years into the future. They realized they would require considerable additional investment to finance growth if they continued operating in the same fashion.

They instituted a series of planned, strategic actions to shrink the Total Business Profile. Actions ranged from price increases and cycle-time reductions in engineering development, manufacturing, and pre-manufacturing activities, to cost reductions in both manufacturing and engineering.

Result: a sharply reduced profile, which allowed a manageable investment to finance strategic growth. Chapter 5 examines this activity in detail.

Cost-Time in Strategic Planning

The most recent development in Westinghouse Cost-Time evolution is called Cash-Conversion Analysis. It was developed by Bill Terzi, now a general consultant at the Westinghouse Productivity and Quality Center.

Cash-Conversion Analysis extends the Cost-Time perspective into strategic decision processes. The analysis is used for such decisions as selecting the best strategy for increasing shareholder value; determining which businesses should

Profile Improvement at One Westinghouse Division

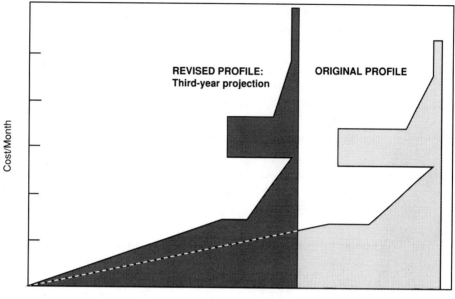

Figure 2-9

Macro Cost-Time Profiles were used by a Westinghouse division to make strategic choices for improvement projects. Revised profile shows the results of carefully chosen actions that significantly reduced investment required to support increased sales and improved profitability.

grow, and which should be divested or acquired; determining how much cash is required to run and grow the business; and establishing acceptable profit levels for each component of the business.

In this analysis the business is viewed as a cash-conversion machine. Insert shareholder cash, "turn the crank" (operate the business), and out comes operating profit. Performance can be measured by the efficiency of the relationship of input to output—how efficiently the business converts shareholder cash to operating profit.

Input and output, both expressed as percentages of sales, are charted as shown in figure 2-10, a Cash-Conversion Efficiency Diagram. Management's performance goal—return on the dynamic investment—is shown as a diagonal

Performance Line. Each business that falls on or near this line is considered equally valuable. It's the ratio that counts—each business on or near the line is generating about the same operating profit percentage return on shareholder cash.

Shrinking the Cost-Time Profile of each component of the business—reducing cycle time and lowering cost—will improve the investment turnover and the operating profit percentage of sales. Further, it will move the Performance Line "northwest" and by definition increase the shareholder value of the business.

The Cash-Conversion Analysis starts with a Cost-Time Profile of each individual product line in the company. These data are aggregated to draw a profile of the entire business (figure 2-11).

Figure 2-12 shows the Cash-Conversion Analysis technique applied to a business unit composed of a large number of individual plants. The Total Business Profile result is plotted as a solid black square, at the centroid of the operations.

Drawing a dashed horizontal Cost Line and a vertical Time Line through the centroid divides the chart into four quadrants and provides a starting point for decision making.

Operations in the northwest quadrant, with above-average return on sales and low-profile cash percent of sales (high investment turnover), are clearly value-enhancing units. Operations in the northeast quadrant are constrained by high cycle time, and need vigorous process-improvement activities. Those in the southwest quadrant are too costly. The units in the southeast or "black hole" quadrant are either "newborn" businesses needed for growth or "sick" businesses, which are a drain on corporate cash and profits, requiring immediate attention.

The direction for increasing value is northwest, and the chart provides a yardstick to evaluate acquisitions, divestitures, and other strategic capital expenditures. The chart also quantifies the amounts of cash needed to grow each segment of the business—in the figure 2-12 example, 52 cents of cash are needed for each dollar of business unit sales growth, unless some significant process changes are made. Finally, by drawing the Performance Line, a management team can quantify where each operation should be in order to attain a specific return on profile cash.

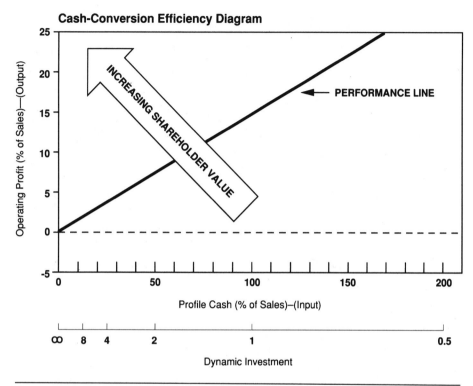

Figure 2-10

Cash-conversion efficiency uses the area of an operation's macro profile to gauge its performance relative to its operating profit. Profile cash (as a percentage of sales) is plotted versus operating profit (as a percentage of sales). This diagrams the relationship of cash input to profit output for each individual product line or divisional component of a business. The arrow indicating increasing shareholder value points to the northwest—the desired direction for all units of a business. The diagonal Performance Line represents management's financial goal—businesses on the same diagonal line are equally valuable regardless of the magnitude of their cash and profit positions. From this point of view, the ratio of profit to cash is what counts.

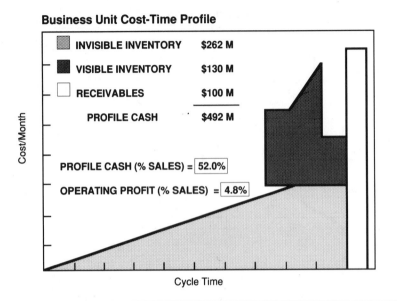

Business Unit Cost-Time Profile

▨ INVISIBLE INVENTORY	$262 M
■ VISIBLE INVENTORY	$130 M
☐ RECEIVABLES	$100 M
PROFILE CASH	$492 M

PROFILE CASH (% SALES) = ⎣ 52.0% ⎦

OPERATING PROFIT (% SALES) = ⎣ 4.8% ⎦

Cost/Month

Cycle Time

Figure 2-11
Calculating profile cash for a business unit requires constructing a macro Cost-Time Profile for the entire business, comprising the weighted sum of the macro profiles of the individual product lines or operations in the unit. In this example, the total cash is $492 million, or 52% of sales. Operating profit for this business is 4.8% of sales. These two data points are plotted on the cash-conversion efficiency diagram together with similar points for all of the individual operations that make up the total organization.

For Westinghouse, Cash-Conversion Analysis adds the element of time and the "invisible inventory" dimension to our strong Value-Based Strategic Management methodologies. It also links strategic considerations directly with day-to-day operations and processes in each segment of the business.

The Cost-Time Perspective

The Cost-Time perspective on business operations accepts the traditional cost perspective and adds some new ideas, as described in the following chart.

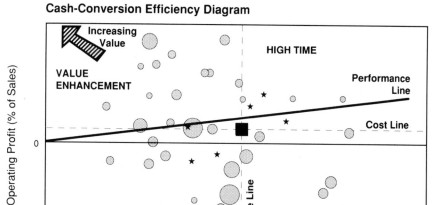

Figure 2-12

Cash-conversion efficiencies for an organization made up of many product lines or plant locations are plotted on the cash-profit diagram. The totals for the entire organization are plotted as a centroid shown here as a solid black square. Profile cash for operating divisions is plotted as stars; the individual plants are shaded circles whose diameters are proportional to sales. This analytical method allows comparisons of the cash-conversion efficiencies for each unit compared to other units, to the total, and to management's targets. The goal is to move all units northwest into the upper-left quadrant—the Value-Enhancement area.

Table 2-1

A Comparison of the Cost Perspective with the Cost-Time Perspective

Cost Perspective	Cost-Time Perspective
Views a business from a cost dimension only.	Views a business from simultaneous cost and time dimensions—with time being equal in importance to cost.
High cost defines areas for improvement.	The Cost-Time Profile identifies and quantifies the "right things" to improve the shareholder value of the business.
Reducing cost increases the shareholder value of the business.	Reducing the cycle time of business processes increases the shareholder value of the business.
Working capital is "visible" and equals inventory plus receivables less payables.	Working capital also includes the invisible inventory—the written-off period costs.
Can quantify the impact of cost reductions on the profitability of the business.	Can also quantify the impact of cycle-time reductions on the profitability of the business.
Operational excellence demands a given return on sales.	Operational excellence demands a simultaneous focus on the return on sales and the investment turnover, including the invisible inventory.

Cost-Time Profiles provide a powerful tool for quantifying the impact of business actions.

For example, a profile allows us to measure directly the impact of reduced cycle time on operational excellence, productivity of capital, and value creation. Viewing period costs as invisible inventory, and as part of working capital allows us to quantify improvement impacts on cash required to run and grow the business.

Measuring value as the return on total capital, including the invisible inventory, can quantify impacts on the income statement and the balance sheet viewed simultaneously. And when shrinking the Cost-Time Profile is regarded as a major Total Quality activity, we can directly measure the impact of Total Quality on cash, operating profit, and value.

This combination of diagnostic and analytical value, along with measurement of areas previously not measurable, makes Cost-Time Profiling a powerful weapon in the competitive arsenal of any business.

The next several chapters describe in detail how to harness this powerful method for your business.

How to Make
and Use Macro
Cost-Time Profiles

The primary purpose of macro Cost-Time Profiles is to better understand the operations of a business, in order to select the most effective areas for improvement. Macro profiles are most useful in diagnosing where to go to work for maximum leverage and return. Micro profiles of the selected areas can then be developed to generate specific improvement projects, as described in chapter 4. Figure 1-3 clarifies this process.

In a formal sense, macro profiles are used to analyze a business to find the best way of increasing shareholder value by impacting the three operational value drivers: operating profit margin, investment turnover, and sales growth.

The most meaningful and effective way to construct the Total Business Macro Profile is to integrate the profiles of lower-level operating units (figure 3-1)— starting with product lines, which aggregate to plants, leading to divisions, which in turn make up the total business. This method also allows the optimum use of Cash-Conversion Analysis for strategic decisions, as discussed in chapter 5.

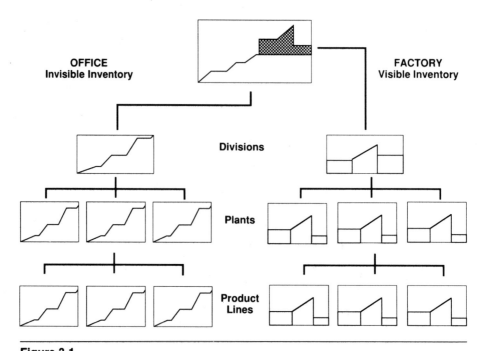

Figure 3-1
The Total Business Macro Cost-Time Profile.

Five sources of data will be needed by the team constructing the macro profile:

- Income statement, without arbitrary allocations.

- Balance sheet, without arbitrary allocations. In most cases, the team will require only data on gross inventory of raw materials and finished parts; work-in-process; and shipping stock; and receivables (product or services delivered and invoiced, but for which payment has not yet been received).

- A flow model, like the one in figure 3-2, showing how information, material, and work flow in the operating unit, from the first concept of a product until the unit collects receivables. For simplicity, our example ignores the possible overlapping between various functions.

- Reasonably accurate weighted cycle times for each of the elements of the flow model.

- Information about the goals and imperatives of the operating unit.

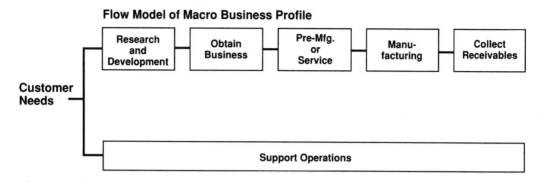

Figure 3-2
Simple flow model of business processes.

The full meaning and use of each of these elements will become clear from the following discussion of how to construct the macro profile. The basic technique is to synthesize three independent macro profiles, then merge them in the correct, weighted time sequence. The three profiles to be constructed and merged are shown in figure 3-3:

- The factory profile (visible inventory)

- The office profile (invisible inventory)

- The receivables profile

We'll look at each profile in turn, then we will deal with their merging.

Constructing a macro profile is a four-step activity:

1. **Obtain business data.**

2. **Develop a flow model of the business.**

3. **Build the Cost-Time Profile.**

4. **Validate the data.**

We'll also take a look at a shortcut method for doing a reasonable, though less-accurate, approximation of this job. Finally, we'll examine ways to use the macro Cost-Time Profile.

Macro Cost-Time Profile

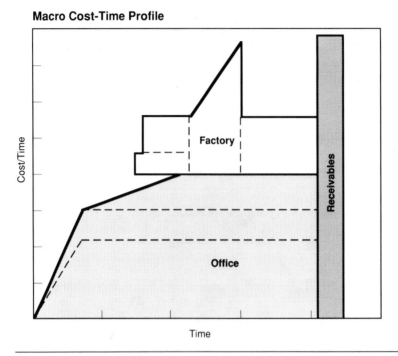

Figure 3-3
The three elements of the macro Cost-Time Profile are the factory, office, and
receivables profiles.

Developing Macro Profiles for
the Factory (Visible Inventory)

1. Obtain operating unit's inventory statement.

The data needed to develop the operating unit's flow model are found on the
year-end average gross inventory control report (figure 3-4 shows a typical
statement).

Our experience at Westinghouse indicates some caution is required in interpreting this statement. Generally, although the gross inventory numbers are correct
from an accounting point of view, we often find the elements—raw material,
finished parts, work-in-process, and shipping stock—are not distributed in a

Inventory Control Report
Year-end Average Month (Dollars in Thousands)

	Actual	Months' Supply
Raw Material	3200	3.2
Finished Parts	2770	4.1
Work-in-Process	11720	3.3
Shipping Stock	4920	4.3
Gross Inventory for Months' Supply	22610	6.4

Figure 3-4
Portion of an inventory control report.

Raw Material: Purchased items on which no labor, except testing or inspecting, is performed prior to placement in raw-material storeroom.

Finished Parts: Raw material to which labor and factory expense have been added and then returned to finished-parts storeroom to be subsequently used in a higher-level assembly.

Work-in-Process: Raw material and finished parts on the factory floor, to which labor and factory expense are added. These costs remain in work-in-process inventory until shipped to finished-parts inventory, customers, or shipping stock.

Shipping Stock: Completed product, self-manufactured or purchased, for customer orders.

way that helps us to create an accurate flow model. There are several reasons for these discrepancies:

- Accounting rules may count all the material in various satellites as work-in-process.

- The rules may count material which is actually work-in-process as finished parts.

- The bookkeeping may not capture time loss between actual physical movement of inventory and the recording of that movement.

These distortions will probably show up during the validation process. To find them and redistribute the gross inventory into its process elements, the team developing the macro profile will need understanding and insight into the business operations.

2. Develop the flow model.

Using the inventory control report (figure 3-4), list the inventory and months' supply for each major inventory category, as well as the total inventory and months' supply. Record the data in some format such as figure 3-5, columns 1 and 2.

Then calculate the inventory issues per month for each category by dividing inventory by months' supply (divide column 1 by column 2). Record the results in column 3.

Using these data, develop the unit's flow model as shown in figure 3-6. All highlighted numbers in this diagram are transferred directly from figure 3-5. To calculate the remaining data, use the following procedures.

- To find Labor and Factory Expense (FE) as an input to Work-in-Process (WIP), simply take the difference between output from WIP and the sum of the inputs from raw materials and finished parts. In figure 3-6, this calculation works out to:

$$\text{Labor and FE (input)} = \$3550/\text{mo.} - (\$1000/\text{mo.} + \$670/\text{mo.})$$
$$= \$1880/\text{mo.}$$

Inventory Control Report

	① Actual ($000)	② Months' Supply	③ Issues/Month
Raw Material	3200	3.2	1000
Finished Parts	2770	4.1	670
Work-in-Process	11720	3.3	3550
Shipping Stock	4920	4.3	1140
Gross Inventory for Months' Supply	22610	6.4	3550

Figure 3-5
Inventory control report with issues per month calculated.

Operating Flow Model

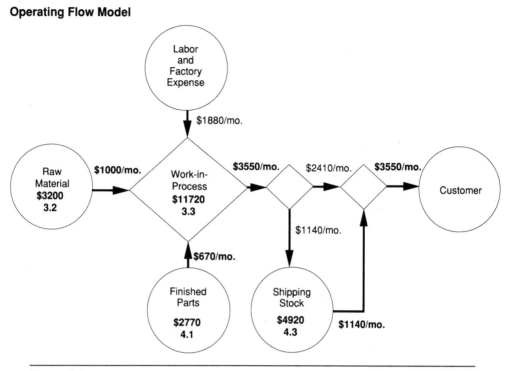

Figure 3-6
Operating-unit flow model (dollars in thousands).

- Shipments to customers are either from shipping stock or directly from work-in-process. Because we know the numbers for shipment from shipping stock ($1140/mo.) and the total shipments to customers ($3550/ mo.), the direct WIP shipment is easily calculated by subtraction. In figure 3-6:

  WIP (shipment) = $3550/mo. − $1140/mo. = $2410/mo.

- The flow from work-in-process to shipping stock (SS) is the difference between the total produced and the amount shipped directly to customers. In figure 3-6:

  WIP to SS = $3550/mo. − $2410/mo. = $1140/mo.

Figure 3-6 diagrams a very simple flow model, adequate for many manufacturing-type businesses. Several factors may complicate the model in some situations. Adding to the flow-model's complexity may be:

- Flows of material to and from satellite operations

- Yield and scrap considerations

- Direct shipments from suppliers to customers

- Purchase resale items

Generally, if these factors are not included at this first stage, they will appear during the validation process and can be corrected for at that time.

3. Develop the Cost-Time Profile.

Two basic equations are used in constructing the macro Cost-Time Profile.

Equation 1

$$\text{Months' supply} = \frac{\text{Inventory}}{\text{Issues/month}}$$

Equation 2

$$\text{Cycle time} = \frac{\text{Months' supply}}{K}$$

where K = a profile factor (see Appendix A). For raw material, finished parts, and shipping stock, $K = 1$.

Using these basic relationships, we will build the macro profile step-by-step.

Profiling finished parts (FP)

From figure 3-6, we know that finished-parts issues are $670 per month and that the months' supply is 4.1. Using equation 2 (and remembering that $K = 1$ in this case):

$$\text{Cycle time (FP)} = \frac{4.1}{1} = 4.1 \text{ months}$$

To plot this part of the profile (figure 3-7), start at cycle time = 0, move upward along the cost axis to $670, then move parallel to the cycle-time axis until you reach 4.1. Then move vertically downward to the cycle-time axis. Label the resulting rectangle Finished Parts.

Profiling raw material (RM)

From figure 3-6, we can see that raw-material issues are $1000 per month and that the months' supply is 3.2. As K = 1 for raw material, we substitute into equation 2:

$$\text{Cycle time (RM)} = \frac{3.2}{1} = 3.2 \text{ months}$$

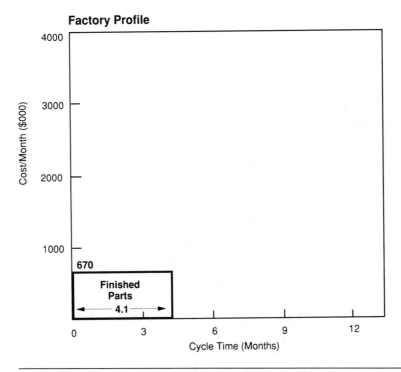

Figure 3-7
Finished-parts segment of the macro factory profile.

To plot the raw-material part of the profile (figure 3-8), start at cycle time = 4.1 and cost = $670. Move upward, parallel to the cost axis, to $1670 (which is $670 + $1000). Then, moving toward the origin and parallel to the cycle-time axis, plot a line equal in length to 3.2 months. Drop a perpendicular from this point to the finished-parts line at cost per month = $670.

Profiling work-in-process (WIP)

Figure 3-6 tells us that the months' supply for work-in-process is 3.3. However, in this case K is not equal to 1. To find K, use the Inventory Worksheet (figure 3-9) and consult Appendix A.

To complete step 1 of the Inventory Worksheet, we need data from figure 3-6. We know that the material input into WIP is $1670 ($1000 + $670), and the output from WIP is $3550. If $3550 is 100% of inventory cost buildup, then

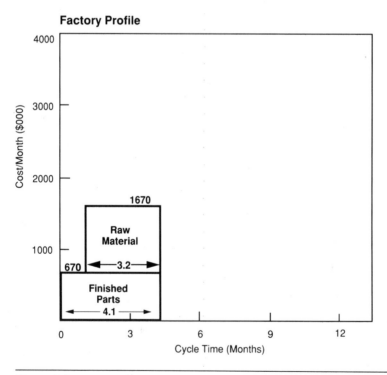

Figure 3-8
Raw-material segment of the macro factory profile.

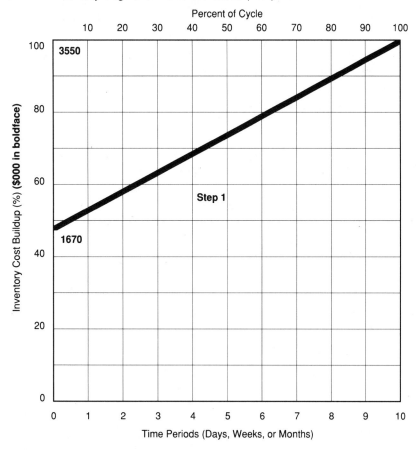

Inventory Worksheet
Inventory Segment: Work-in-Process (WIP)

Step 2

Profile K Factor = <u>Number of blocks under curve</u> = <u>75</u> = | 0.75 |
Total number of blocks   100

Figure 3-9
Inventory Worksheet to determine K Factor.

material input ($1670) is 47% of inventory cost buildup. Drawing a line from 47% (on the cost axis) to the point of 100% of cost and 100% of cycle time provides the remaining data. Step 2 of figure 3-9 calculates the Factor to be K = 0.75.

Now we can substitute the months' supply and K Factor data in equation 2:

$$\text{Cycle time (WIP)} = \frac{3.3}{0.75} = 4.5 \text{ months}$$

Drawing the work-in-process profile segment (figure 3-10) simply involves plotting a diagonal line from the point at cycle time = 4.1 and cost per month = $1670 to a point 4.5 months later when cost per month = $3550, and dropping a perpendicular from this point to the horizontal axis.

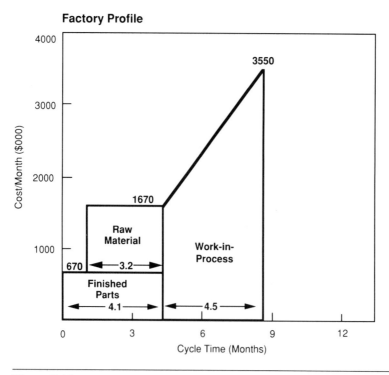

Figure 3-10

Work-in-process segment of the macro factory profile.

Profiling shipping stock (SS)

Shipping stock issues in figure 3-6 are $1140 per month, and the input into shipping stock from work-in-process is also $1140 per month. Shipping stock months' supply is 4.3, and K = 1. Equation 2 yields:

$$\text{Cycle time (SS)} = \frac{4.3}{1} = 4.3 \text{ months}$$

To plot the shipping stock profile (figure 3-11), begin at the point where the WIP line ended. Move down, parallel to the cost axis, to $1140; move right, parallel to the time axis for 4.3 months; then drop a perpendicular to the time axis.

The unit's Cost-Time Profile for the factory (visible inventory) is now complete (figure 3-11).

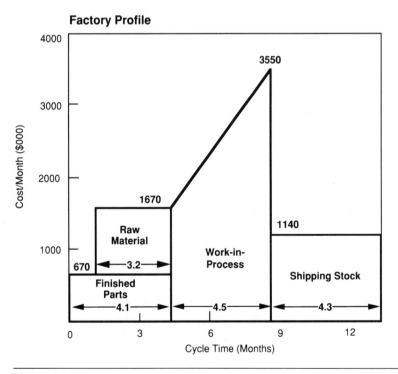

Figure 3-11
Completed factory portion of macro Cost-Time Profile, including shipping-stock segment.

4. Validate the flow model and Cost-Time Profile.

Our experience has shown that it is mandatory to validate the flow model and the Cost-Time Profile, because they are the foundations for selecting areas in which to improve the business operation. Several factors may impact the quality and accuracy of data.

- The inventory control report may not correctly segregate the gross inventory into its component parts (as reflected in figure 3-5).

- Other factors may impact the complexity of the flow model. These generally come to light during the validation step.

- Acquiring the data for this macro view process is often a laborious task, involving sifting through information which is not readily available. Thus, the team compiling the macro profile is sometimes tempted to terminate the process prematurely and use grossly approximate data. While absolute accuracy is not required, the data must at least be credible.

Validation consists of comparing the data used in the flow model and profile with data obtained from other independent sources. If agreement is close, then the charted data are credible. In general, the data-gathering process will be effective in proportion to the team's basic understanding of the business and their tenacity in sifting data.

Figure 3-12 suggests some guidelines for validating the flow model and the Cost-Time Profile. The objective is to ensure we are modeling the "real world." The method is to compare data from the balance sheet with the same data available from the income statement and other financial data. If deviations are within acceptable limits, the data are regarded as valid.

If the flow model and the Cost-Time Profile cannot be reconciled, return to step 1 "Obtain operating units inventory statement" and start the process again, applying the necessary understanding and insight into the business to better segregate the gross inventory into its component parts. This iteration is needed to evolve a flow model of the business operation that is closer to reality.

Validation Guidelines

A. Flow Model, figure 3-6   **Source of Data**

    1. Flow to customer   = $3550 / mo.   Figure 3-6

$$= \frac{\text{Yearly Sales} \times \text{Inventory Ratio}}{12}$$ Income Statement

    Do the two numbers agree?

    2. Flow to customer from SS = $1140 / mo. = 32%   Figure 3-6
       Flow to customer from WIP = $2410 / mo. = 68%   Figure 3-6

    Are these percentages compatible with reality?   Financial Data

    3. Flow of labor and factory expense   = $1880 / mo.   Figure 3-6
         into WIP   = Net Allowed Hours / mo.
                                × Costing Rate   Financial Data

    Do the two numbers agree?

    4. Flow of RM into WIP = $1000 / mo.   Figure 3-6

    Is this number compatible with raw-material purchases?   Purchasing Data

    5. Flow of FP into WIP = $670 / mo.   Figure 3-6

    Is the number compatible with finished-parts purchases?   Purchasing Data

B. Factory Cost-Time Profile, figure 3-11

    The area of each segment of the profile should agree with the inventory data shown in figure 3-6.

    • Raw-material area   = $3200
    • Finished-parts area   = $2700
    • Work-in-process area   = $11720
    • Shipping-stock area   = $4920

Figure 3-12

A reality check: validation guidelines for the factory macro profile.

Looking Deeper into Raw Material and Finished Parts Profiles

A more detailed macro profile of raw material or finished parts can sometimes help in analyzing areas of particular concern.

For example, refer to figure 3-8. The raw material profile is shown as a rectangle with issues per month of $1,000,000 and a 3.2 months' supply. Assume that raw material has three components: steel, copper, and aluminum. Use a worksheet similar to that shown in figure 3-13 to aggregate the profile data.

In figure 3-13, the second and third columns tabulate, for each commodity, the percentage usage per month and the average months' supply—or cycle time— of each one. To compute the weighted cycle time (the fourth column) for each element, multiply the percentage of usage per month by the months' supply and divide by 100.

In our example, this procedure yields a weighted months' supply of 3.2, which agrees with our previous calculation in figure 3-8.

Detailed Look at Raw Material

Elements of Raw Material	% Usage per Month	Months' Supply	% Usage per month × Months Supply
Steel	60	2.4	145
Copper	25	4.0	100
Aluminum	15	5.0	75
Weighted Total	100	3.2	320

Figure 3-13
Raw material considerations.

To construct the profiles for each commodity (figure 3-14), begin with the element having the longest cycle time—in our case, aluminum. Plot its cycle time (5 months) on the horizontal axis and its percentage usage per month (15%) on the vertical axis, defining a rectangle. Repeat this process cumulatively, in descending cycle-time order, to obtain the rectangles for the other commodities.

The area of the resulting profile is still $3,200,000, identical to the area shown in figure 3-8. Now, however, our analysis allows us to identify specific areas for concentrating our improvement efforts.

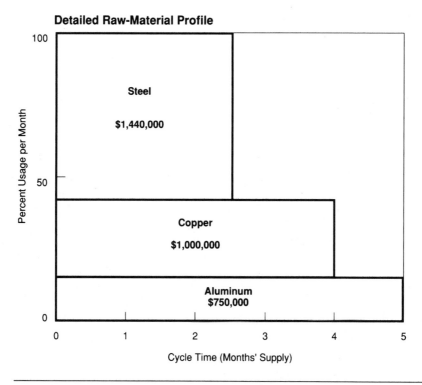

Figure 3-14
Detailed raw-material profile.

Developing Macro Profiles for the Office (Invisible Inventory)

Constructing the macro profile for office activities is similar to building the macro profile for the factory. Somewhat different data sources are used, but the procedure is the same.

1. Obtain the income statement.

We'll develop cost data for the flow model from the unit's year-end average monthly income statement (figure 3-15 shows an example).

2. Develop the flow model.

The flow model is a block diagram of the business processes involved in converting a customer need into a billable product or service. Processes that might be incorporated into such a model could include:

Obtain business	Subcontract work
Process orders	Estimate costs
Plan resources	Monitor performance
Obtain material	Manage project
Produce product or	Supervise construction
provide service	Develop product or service
Distribute product	Verify design
Install system	Support operations
Design system	Install product
Collect receivables	

To build a flow model of your operation, define the processes that apply to your unit and organize them into sequential order. Be aware that in most organizations these processes involve overlap between functions. For simplicity, we are ignoring the overlap.

Figure 3-16 presents a simple, generic flow model including five processes.

Average Monthly Income Statement

	($000)
Sales and Other Revenue	$7880
Transportation Cost	94
Compensation on Sales & Cash Discount	79
Direct Cost—Labor	783
Direct Cost—Material	1670
Direct Cost—Factory Expense	660
Customer Order Development—Shop	125
Engineering Contracts	719
Product Warranty	50
Other	371
Manufacturing	437
Engineering	180
Marketing	385
Administrative and General	474
Other	223
Strategic Managed Costs	358
Research and Development	44
Depreciation and Lease Cost	423
Insurance & Taxes—Holidays & Vacations	190
Inventory Change Effect on Income before Taxes	9
Headquarters Selling Costs	106
Corporate Managed Costs	158
Total Cost of Sales	7538
Operating Profit	342

Figure 3-15
Example of an income statement.

Obtain Business includes the processes of marketing, negotiating and selling. Cost may include personnel from other functions such as engineering and manufacturing.

Pre-Manufacturing or Service includes the remaining processes that have a direct impact on completion of the product or service, such as engineering, drafting, or purchasing.

Manufacturing includes all the processes of the factory.

Flow Model

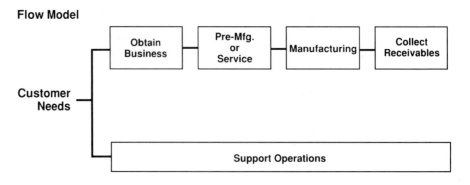

Figure 3-16
Business-operations flow model, ignoring overlaps and R&D.

Support Operations encompass the remaining
business processes that have no direct impact
on completion of the product or service,
including human resources, finance, and general and administrative activities.

Collect Receivables is the process of collecting
the customers' unpaid bills.

3. Develop the Cost-Time Profile.

Constructing the Cost-Time Profile for the office (invisible inventory) is a
three-step process.

    a. Develop cost data for each process in the flow model.

    b. Determine the weighted cycle time for each process in the flow model.

    c. Construct the Cost-Time Profile.

a. Develop cost data.

Obtain cost data for the processes of the flow model from the income statement
(figure 3-15). Using this statement as a basis, enter each flow-model process as
a column heading and include a Sales and Revenue column (figure 3-17). Next,
apportion the cost data from each line of the income statement to the business
processes. To do this properly, the team must have a good understanding of the

Average Monthly Income Statement

	($000)	A Support Oper	B Obtain Bus	C Pre-Mfg or Svc	D Mfg Matl	E Mfg Lab	F Sls & Rev	G Coll Rec
Sales and Other Revenue	$7880						7880	7880
Transportation Cost	94	94						
Compensation on Sales & Cash Discount	79	79						
Direct Cost—Labor	783					783		
Direct Cost—Material	1670				1670			
Direct Cost—Factory Expense	660					660		
Customer Order Development—Shop	125			125				
Engineering Contracts	719			719				
Product Warranty	50	50						
Other	371	371						
Manufacturing	437					437		
Engineering	180			180				
Marketing	385		385					
Administrative and General	474	474						
Other	223	223						
Strategic Managed Costs	358	358						
Research and Development	44	44						
Depreciation and Lease Cost	423	423						
Insurance & Taxes—Holidays & Vacations	190	190						
Inventory Change Effect on Income before Taxes	9	9	106					
Headquarters Selling Costs	106							
Corporate Managed Costs	158	158						
Total Cost of Sales	7538							
Operating Profit	342							
a) Total Cost; Revenue		2473	491	1024	1670	1880	7880	7880
b) Cycle Time (Months)								
c) Cumulative Cost; Revenue		2473	2964	3988	5658	7538	7880	7880
d) Cumulative Weighted Cycle Time (Months)								

Figure 3-17

Income statement distributed by business process and showing cost numbers (lines "a" and "c").

functional relationships and interactions within the unit being profiled. Then total the costs, both individually for each process (line "a" at the bottom) and cumulatively (line "c").

b. Determine weighted cycle times.

Obtaining reasonably accurate weighted cycle times for each process in the flow model is the most challenging part of Cost-Time Profiling. Most companies simply don't keep the books that way. The Cost-Time methodology recognizes that time data will be far less accurate than cost data, which are normally kept to several decimal places.

The data we need to measure is the average elapsed time to complete a process. Incredible though it seems, most businesses have no idea of the cycle time for their processes—which makes it quite difficult to manage those processes!

Note that "elapsed time" is very different from "hands-on" time. For the total business—including all the backlogs, queues, and waits—the elapsed time may be 100 to 1,000 times longer than the hands-on time.

To get a start on estimating the elapsed time of a process, examine the planning and scheduling records of the operation. Then ask people involved in the process a series of questions, and perform the calculations or make the estimates indicated.

- For **Obtain Business** cycle time, ask: **"From the first glimmer of interest by the potential customer, how long on the average does it take until an order is entered?"**

- **For Pre-Manufacturing or Service** cycle time, ask: "When one of the orders entered is released, how long on the average will it take to complete the office functions?"

- For **Manufacturing** cycle time, ask: **"How long on the average does it take from the release of purchase orders until the product is shipped?"** From the perspective of the office profile, this period is waiting time—essentially, wasted time.

- For **Collect Receivables** cycle time, divide the gross receivables by the monthly sales (assuming the monthly billings are essentially equal to the monthly sales). The result will be a fair approximation of the cycle time for collect receivables.

- For **Support Operations,** which have no direct impact on completion of a product or service, the cycle time is not on the critical path. Each unit must develop its own estimated value for it. The most commonly used estimate—which we use in our example—is to equate the cycle time for support with the cycle time of the first process (in our example, the obtain-business process).

To weight the cycle times, one popular technique uses sales volume as the weighting factor. Multi-product businesses (in which different products have different cycles) will need to calculate a single, weighted cycle time for each process.

Figure 3-18 illustrates a business that has three product lines—A, B, and C. The product lines represent, respectively, 50%, 30%, and 20% of sales, with cycle times of 12, 6, and 2 months. As shown, to compute the weighted cycle time of the Obtain Business process, multiply the percentage of sales of each

Obtain Business

PRODUCT	% SALES	CYCLE TIME	% SALES × CYCLE TIME
A	50	12	600
B	30	6	180
C	20	2	40
Weighted Total	100	8.2	820

Figure 3-18
Weighted cycle times of the Obtain Business process.

product by its cycle time, aggregate the total, and divide by 100—yielding a weighted cycle time of 8.2 months.

Similarly, calculate the weighted cycle times for each of the remaining business processes. For our example, these weighted cycle times are shown at the bottom of figure 3-19, individually in line "b"; and cumulatively in line "d."

c. Construct the Cost-Time Profile.

Figure 3-19 now contains all the data required to construct the macro Cost-Time Profile of the office. Figure 3-20 shows our sample profile.

Start by drawing a dotted line from the origin (0,0) to the cumulative cost-time coordinates of Support operations (2473,3). Because Support continues regardless of product activities, go back to the origin (0,0) and draw another line (solid) to the cumulative cost-time coordinates of Obtain Business (2964,3), which is the first process in the direct processes influencing product or service completion. From that point (2964,3), draw a solid line to the cumulative cost-time coordinates of the next process in line, Pre-Manufacturing or Service (3988,11).

The office functions have now been profiled. If this were a service operation, the macro profile would now be complete except for the Collect Receivables process, which would be constructed from this point onward. We will deal with receivables profiling later in this chapter.

Because our example is of a manufacturing operation, however, we must portray the effects of the office waiting period while the factory makes the product. According to figure 3-19, the weighted cycle time for manufacture is 10 months (cost of manufacture does not impact this profile, as it is included in the manufacturing profile). At the top of the profile draw a horizontal line extending 10 months. This line represents the factory process time and implies that during this time the office has no interaction with the factory and, hence, incurs no cost. This is a useful simplifying assumption. Drop a perpendicular to the time axis, extend horizontal lines from the coordinates for the Support

Average Monthly Income Statement

	($000)	A Support Oper	B Obtain Bus	C Pre-Mfg or Svc	D Mfg Matl	E Mfg Lab	F Sls & Rev	G Coll Rec
Sales and Other Revenue	$7880						7880	7880
Transportation Cost	94	94						
Compensation on Sales & Cash Discount	79	79						
Direct Cost—Labor	783					783		
Direct Cost—Material	1670				1670			
Direct Cost—Factory Expense	660					660		
Customer Order Development—Shop	125			125				
Engineering Contracts	719			719				
Product Warranty	50	50						
Other	371	371						
Manufacturing	437					437		
Engineering	180			180				
Marketing	385		385					
Administrative and General	474	474						
Other	223	223						
Strategic Managed Costs	358	358						
Research and Development	44	44						
Depreciation and Lease Cost	423	423						
Insurance & Taxes—Holidays & Vacations	190	190						
Inventory Change Effect On Income before Taxes	9	9						
Headquarters Selling Costs	106		106					
Corporate Managed Costs	158	158						
Total Cost of Sales	7538							
Operating Profit	342							

		A	B	C	D	E	F	G
a) Total Cost; Revenue		2473	491	1024	1670	1880	7880	7880
b) Cycle Time (Months)		–	3	8	◄ 10 ►			1.5
c) Cumulative Cost; Revenue		2473	2964	3988	5658	7538	7880	7880
d) Cumulative Weighted Cycle Time (Months)		3	3	11	◄ 21 ►		21	22.5

Figure 3-19

Income statement showing cycle-time numbers (lines "b" and "d").

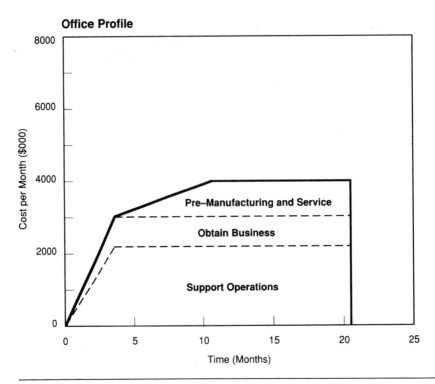

Figure 3-20
Office portion of macro Cost-Time Profile.

and Obtain Business processes over to the endpoint (for clarity), and the Cost-Time Profile is complete.

4. Validate the flow model and Cost-Time Profile.

The flow model for office processes and the resulting Cost-Time Profile are validated by a consensus among key staff of the unit that the model is a reasonable portrayal of reality. For the flow model and profile to be useful, the key staff must agree on all of the following:

- The flow model and profile accurately depict how information, material, and work flow in the unit, from first customer inquiry until receivables are collected

- The cost allocations to the various processes are reasonably accurate

- The weighted cycle times of the various processes are fair representations of reality

Developing Macro Profiles for the Receivables

Completing the macro Cost-Time Profile involves constructing a macro profile for receivables. This is a simple calculation so long as monthly billings are essentially equal to monthly sales.

To plot the receivables profile, we need to know monthly sales and receivables cycle time. Determine the monthly sales from the income statement, figure 3-19. In our example this is $7,880,000.

To determine the cycle time, first obtain the total dollar amount of receivables from the balance sheet. In our example, assume this to be $11,820,000. To find weighted cycle time (or months' supply of receivables), divide receivables by monthly sales:

$$\text{Cycle time} = \frac{11,820,000}{7,880,000} = 1.5 \text{ months}$$

Figure 3-21 shows the macro profile for receivables. It is a rectangle with height equal to monthly sales and width equal to the cycle time. Its area is equal to the dollar amount of receivables.

Looking Deeper into Receivables

If receivables is a major area of concern, it may be worthwhile to construct a more detailed macro profile. The overall profile shown in figure 3-21 can be segmented into various elements, including:

Current—due in the current month

Deferred—not due within current month based on terms of sale

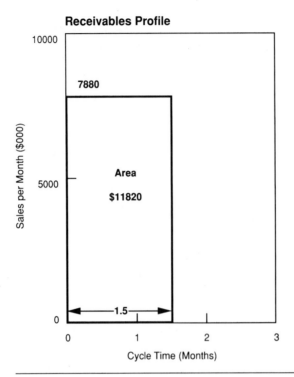

Figure 3-21
Receivables portion of macro Cost-Time Profile.

Overdue—not paid by due date

Suspended—customer refuses to pay because of an identified problem

Legal—legal action taken because of non-payment by customer

Use a worksheet similar to the one shown in figure 3-22 to aggregate the profile data. The second and third columns tabulate, for each element of receivables, the percentage of billings each represents and the average months' supply—or cycle time—of each element.

To compute the weighted cycle times (the fourth column), multiply the percentage of billings by the cycle time for each element, and divide by 100. In our

A Detailed Look at Receivables

Elements of Receivables	% Billings	Cycle Time	% Billings × Cycle Time
Current	83	1	83
Deferred	5	2	10
Overdue	7	3	21
Suspense	3	4	12
Legal	2	12	24
Weighted Total	100	1.5	150

Figure 3-22
A detailed look at receivables helps identify needed improvements.

example, this method yields a weighted cycle time of 1.5 months, which agrees with our previous calculation.

To construct the detailed profiles for receivables (figure 3-23), start with the element having the longest cycle time—in our case, "Legal." Plot its cycle time (12 months) on the horizontal axis and its percentage billings (2%) on the vertical axis, defining a rectangle. Repeat the process cumulatively, in descending cycle-time order.

The area of the resulting profile is still $11,820,000—identical to the area in figure 3-21. In this case, however, the detailed analysis allows us to identify specific targets within receivables for our improvement activities.

Integrating the Factory, Office, and Receivables Profiles

Thus far, we have constructed separate macro Cost-Time Profiles for the factory (figure 3-11), the office (figure 3-20), and receivables (figure 3-21).

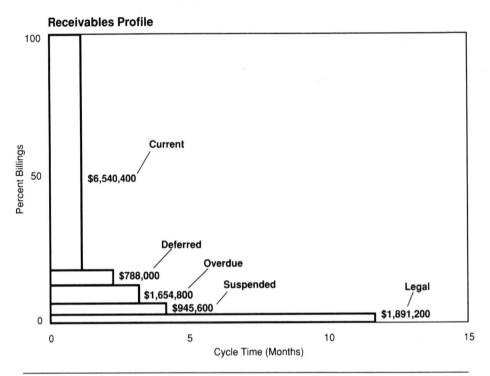

Figure 3-23
Detailed profile of receivables.

Integrating them into a single Total Business Profile is largely a matter of drawing them on the same scale in proper relationship (figure 3-24).

Start the office profile at the origin (0,0). Place the receivables profile so its time axis continues the office profile's time line and its vertical axis coincides with the right-hand edge of the office profile. Now place the factory profile so its time axis coincides with the top line of the office profile and its right-hand edge abuts the receivables profile.

We now have a Total Business Macro Cost-Time Profile. Interpreting the profile and putting it to use are covered below, in the section titled "How to Use the Macro Cost-Time Profile."

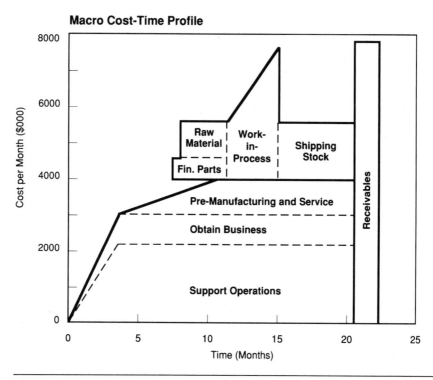

Figure 3-24
Completed macro Cost-Time Profile.

An Alternate Method for
Building Factory Profiles

The shortcut method for constructing factory macro profiles uses income state-ment data instead of balance sheet data, to determine the flow of labor and material. The profile construction is quicker and simpler—but considerable portions of the learning experience are lost in the process. For the fullest understanding of the business and the ability to translate the profile into action plans, the team building the macro profile should follow the longer method outlined earlier in this chapter.

For the following example, which summarizes the shorter method of constructing factory profiles, we have arranged the numbers so the results of the two
methods will be virtually identical. In practice, this is an unlikely outcome.
Therefore, validation of the flow model and Cost-Time Profile remains essential.

1. Calculate the raw material and finished parts profile.

In the inventory control report (figure 3-4), the raw material (RM) and finished
parts (FP) inventory is:

$$RM + FP = \$3200 + \$2770 = \$5970$$

From the income statement (figure 3-19), column D, the material flow per
month is $1670. Thus:

$$\text{Cycle time (RM + FP)} = \frac{\text{Inventory}}{\text{Flow}} = \frac{5970}{1670} = 3.6 \text{ months}$$

Figure 3-25 shows the raw material and finished parts macro profile.

2. Calculate the work-in-process profile.

The inventory control report (figure 3-4) shows that the work-in-process inventory is $11,720. The income statement (figure 3-19), column E, line "a," lists
labor plus overhead flow per month as $1880.

Using these data we can construct a trapezoid to represent the work-in-process
profile (figure 3-26). We can find the cycle time (t) from simple geometry
because we know the area of the trapezoid: it is WIP inventory or $11,720.
Using the formula for the area of a trapezoid, and substituting our data:

$$11720 = (1670) (t) + 1/2 (1880) (t)$$

thus $t = 4.5$ months

We can now plot our trapezoid (figure 3-26) with 4.5 months as the cycle time
and a height of $1670 + 1880 = 3550$ for the cost axis.

3. Calculate the shipping stock macro profile.

From the inventory control report (figure 3-4), we know the shipping stock
inventory is $4920. To determine the flow into and out of shipping stock:

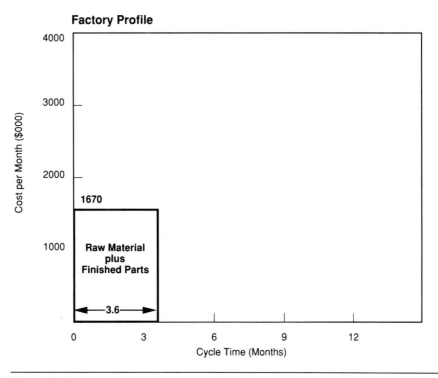

Figure 3-25
Shortcut factory macro profile—raw material and finished parts segment.

a. Assume that, on the average, the flow into shipping stock equals the outflow.

b. Determine the percentage of factory output which, on the average, is delivered to customers as order-for-order; also determine the percentage of factory output destined for shipping stock. In our example, the breakdown is 68% delivered to the customer and 32% delivered to shipping stock.

Because we know that factory output is $3550 per month (figure 3-26), we can immediately calculate the output delivered to shipping stock (SS) per month: it's $3550 times 32% = $1140. And so:

$$\text{Cycle time (SS)} = \frac{\text{Inventory}}{\text{Flow}} = \frac{4920}{1140} = 4.3 \text{ months}$$

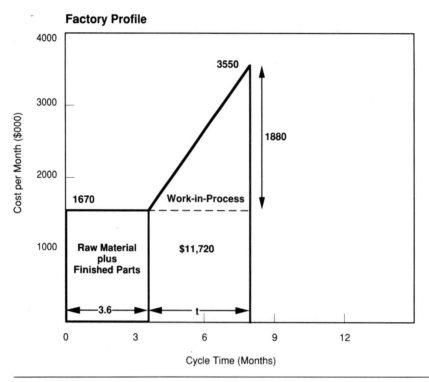

Figure 3-26
Shortcut factory macro profile—work-in-process segment.

Plot the result as shown in figure 3-27. We have completed the factory (visible inventory) macro Cost-Time Profile.

To repeat the previous warning: the shortcut method of building a factory profile is a convenient approximation; it is essential for the team to validate the profile before using it to make decisions!

How to Use the Macro Cost-Time Profile

Macro Cost-Time Profiles are used to identify specific areas of the business operations which, if improved, will contribute significant increases to shareholder value by impacting the operating value drivers of operating profit margin,

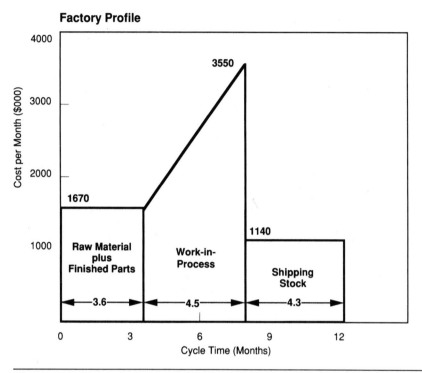

Figure 3-27
Shortcut factory macro profile completed, including shipping-stock segment.

investment turnover, and sales growth. As figure 3-28 shows, shrinking the macro profile directly impacts both operating profit margin and investment turnover by improving cost or reducing cycle time, or both. Our experience also shows that profile-slimming improves quality, reduces time to market, and enhances customer service—all of which contribute significantly to sales growth.

The result of the macro profile analysis is a selection of improvement projects aimed at specific processes. The macro profile provides a direct link between individual improvement projects, described by micro profiles shown in chapter 4, and the financial results of the operation. This linkage is described in figure 3-29. The figure shows how individual processes are aggregated into product-line profiles, which in turn are clustered into plant (site) profiles that make up the Total Business Profile. Because the entire hierarchy of profiles is quantitative,

Objective: Shrink the Business Profile

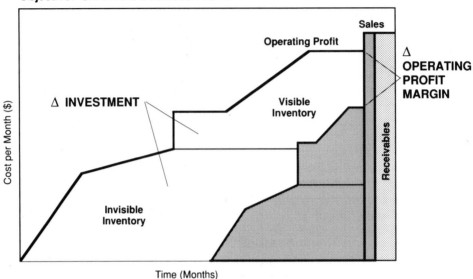

Figure 3-28
Shrinking the business profile (goal is to reach size of shaded portion of profile).

this ladder—from sub-process micro profiles all the way up to the Total Business (macro) Profile—allows managers to calculate directly the effects on the business of improving individual processes and sub-processes.

An example of this type of calculation is illustrated in Chapter 5. That chapter also introduces the concept of Cash-Conversion Efficiency, which extends the use of macro profiles into the realm of strategic decisions including acquisitions and divestitures, strategic-growth investments, cash-flow considerations, and profit-level acceptability.

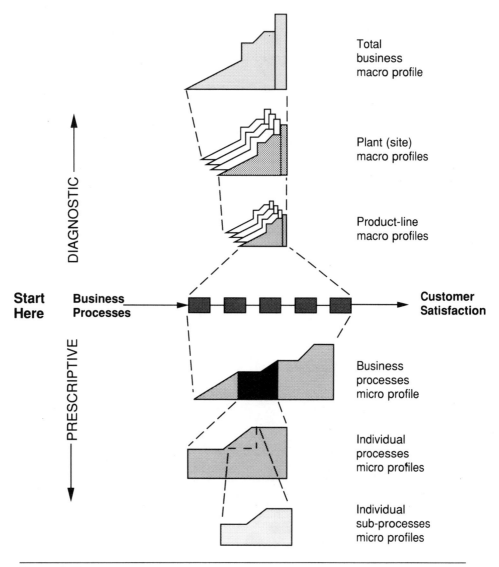

Figure 3-29
Macro profiles (above the Start Here line) have been described in chapter 3; micro profiles (below the Start Here line) are discussed in chapter 4.

How to Make
and Use Micro
Cost-Time Profiles

Constructing Cost-Time Profiles—and determining improvement plans based on them—requires a **process-oriented view** of business activities. All work is accomplished through processes. We define a process as a sequence of work activities which is repeatable and measurable.

This point of view is familiar in the factory because manufacturing processes have usually been analyzed thoroughly to determine cost structures. In the office, the process view may be less familiar. In Westinghouse experience, though, the analysis is easy to do once the concept is understood.

As described in chapter 1 and as seen in figure 3-29, profiling can be used at any level of detail. From the macro Cost-Time Profile, the quality improvement team can diagnose which area or function needs to be analyzed in greater detail. The micro cost-time profile charts the collection of process-activity costs over the elapsed cycle time for one unit of service or product. Besides diagnosing the areas for improvement, the team can prescribe effective actions because the micro cost-time profile is detailed and specific—excessive costs and excessive cycle times are clear and visible.

As a rule of thumb, we begin with the broadest-reaching process discovered in the macro profile and develop its micro profile. If this effort produces useful improvement ideas, we proceed with them. If not, we select the areas of the micro profile most in need of improvement, and develop additional detailed profiles of those areas. We have included profiling techniques for both high-level processes and detailed activities in this chapter.

Constructing the micro Cost-Time Profile is a four-step activity:

1. **Construct a flow diagram.**
2. **Develop cost data and prepare flow diagram with costs.**
3. **Develop elapsed time data and prepare Time-Cycle Chart.**
4. **Construct micro Cost-Time Profile.**

This basic four-step approach is diagrammed in figure 4-1. It's universally applicable to any area or function of a business—the factory, the office, or the field.

In this chapter we'll first develop a micro profile for an office process. At the end of the chapter we'll examine how the same technique applies to factory processes. Most important, we'll discuss how to interpret the profiles, and we'll develop specific action-agendas for improvement, including specific ways to measure results.

These activities are normally done by employee task teams, composed of people involved in the processes being analyzed. Throughout the next section, we will furnish tips and ideas for helping those teams to be as productive as possible, using the Cost-Time methodology. A typical Cost-Time effort, from making the initial investigation through developing a detailed improvement-project plan, takes an elapsed time of from five to eight weeks to complete, with a team working on a part-time basis.

Developing an Office Micro Profile

Generally, in a Total Quality activity, the critical processes—the ones that must improve if the business is to achieve greater success—have been identified as

How to Construct a Micro Cost-Time Profile

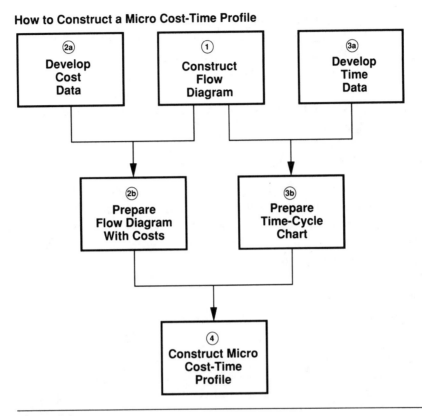

Figure 4-1
The four-step process for constructing micro Cost-Time Profiles.

part of the macro profile diagnostic process described in chapter 3. Micro profiles are then used to examine the appropriate processes in detail. There are many office processes and functions for an improvement team to choose from, such as:

Obtain business	Subcontract work
Process orders	Estimate costs
Plan resources	Monitor performance
Obtain material	Manage project
Produce product or	Supervise construction
provide service	Develop product or service

Distribute product   Verify design
Install system   Support operations
Design system   Install product
Collect receivables

For this example we will use the Obtain Business process (shown as the first block in figure 3-16).

1. Construct the flow diagram.

The first step of the analysis is to identify the major activities of the process or function being studied and to determine their sequential relationship. This can be displayed as a flow diagram. Although office activities often overlap, they should be shown as sequential blocks. Figure 4-2 shows a flow diagram for the function Obtain Business.

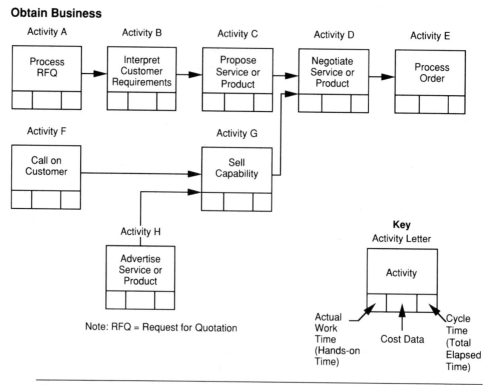

Figure 4-2
Micro flow diagram for the office function Obtain Business.

2. Develop cost data.

Cost data will take the form of cost per activity (for each block in the flow diagram). These data can be derived from the portion of the operating budget attributed to the function being analyzed.

We developed a cost-distribution form (figure 4-3) to help distribute the budgets to the activities on the flow diagram. These activities are listed across the top (right side) of the form. The columns should also include (left side):

- A budget identification number for each participating organizational unit

- The total monthly budget

- The percentage of the total budget applicable to the activities on the flow diagram

- The number of work units (in this example, orders) processed per month

- The budgeted dollars per work unit per month, obtained by dividing the portion of the budget applicable to those activities by the number of work units processed per month; distribute these dollars across the listed activities

Obtain Business

Budget No.	Total Budget (Month)	% of Budget	Units per Month	Budget Allocated per Unit †	A Process RFQ	B Interpret Customer Reqmnts	C Propose Svc or Product	D Negotiate Svc or Product	E Process Order	F Call on Customer	G Sell Capability	H Advertise Svc or Product
4120	$157K	25	100	$393	$98		$247		$48			
4180	358K	65	100	2327		$233	349	$663	384	$349	$233	$116
8150	325K	50	100	1625		243		325	894		163	
			Totals	$4345	$98	$476	$596	$988	$1326	$349	$396	$116

† Budget Allocated per Unit = $\dfrac{\text{Total Budget (Month)} \times \text{\% of Budget}}{\text{Units Per Month}}$

Note: RFQ = Request for Quotation

Figure 4-3
Cost-distribution form (data for flow diagram).

These data will not be exact, and we find that knowledgeable approximations are quite sufficient to yield excellent results in this area. When the team is satisfied that the cost distribution is fairly representative, they can total the costs per work unit and enter them in the cost block for each activity on the flow diagram (figure 4-4).

3. Prepare the Time-Cycle Chart.

Estimate the total elapsed time (cycle time) required for a work unit (an order, a design, a batch of invoices, etc.) to flow through each activity. The cycle time begins when the work arrives at the work station (or when it leaves the prior work station). The cycle includes both performance of the work and any queue time, and ends when the work leaves the work station.

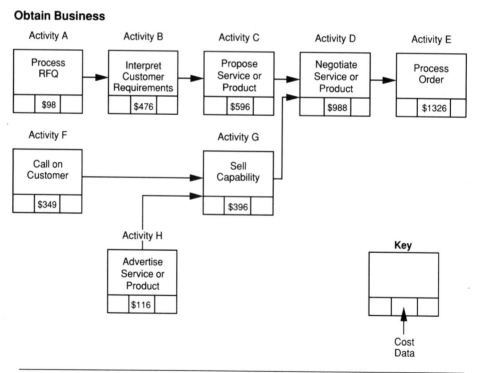

Figure 4-4
Micro flow diagram with cost data.

You can obtain this information from schedules, from estimates made by the function manager or the people who perform the activities, or through measurement. One way to estimate cycle time is first to determine how many units are in-process or waiting to be done. Then to obtain the cycle time, divide the normal rate at which the units are finished into the number of work units in-process or waiting. Depending on the activity, the time may be measured in minutes, hours, or days. Enter this total elapsed time to perform the activity in the lower right-hand block of each activity in the flow diagram (figure 4-5).

Next, prepare a Time-Cycle Chart (figure 4-6) by plotting the elapsed times for each activity along a time scale, moving from right to left. The starting point (at zero) represents delivery to the customer—external or internal—the next

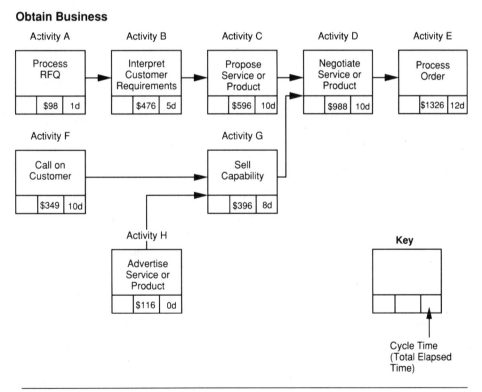

Figure 4-5
Micro flow diagram with cost and cycle-time data.

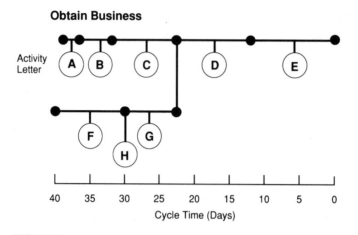

Figure 4-6
Time-Cycle Chart used in constructing a micro Cost-Time Profile. Activity letters
label the lines between the dots.

person or group in line. Branches of the Time-Cycle Chart mirror those on the
flow diagram, except they will now be in time relationship as well as in
activity-flow relationship. To help identify each activity, place the activity
letter from the flow diagram below the line representing the cycle time of that
activity.

4. Construct the micro Cost-Time Profile.

Using the cost data from the flow diagram and the cycle time from the Time-
Cycle Chart, construct the micro Cost-Time Profile.

There are two types of micro profiles, depending on whether the activities are
performed in a series or are performed in parallel. If the activities have a
straight-through flow (figure 4-7), the Cost-Time Profile will be similar to the
one in figure 4-8. If the activities occur in parallel, as shown in figure 4-5, the
profile will be similar to figure 4-9. This profile consists of series profiles for
each leg of the flow diagram, stacked at common junctures.

Construction of both the series and parallel profiles is the same. The cost for
each activity, written on the flow diagram, is considered as being equally
distributed over the cycle time for the activity. Figure 4-8 shows an easy way

Obtain Business

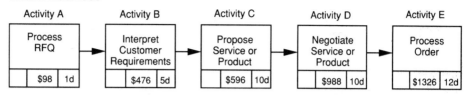

Note: RFQ = Request for Quotation

Figure 4-7
Micro flow diagram showing business activities occurring in series (straight-through flow).

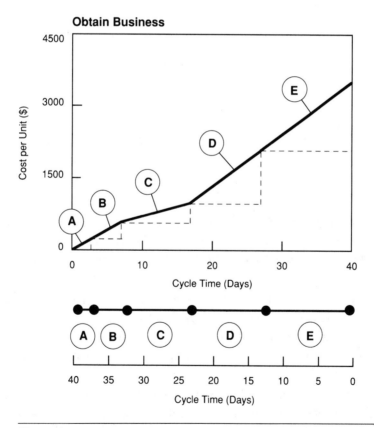

Figure 4-8
Micro Series Cost-Time Profile for business activities occurring in a series.

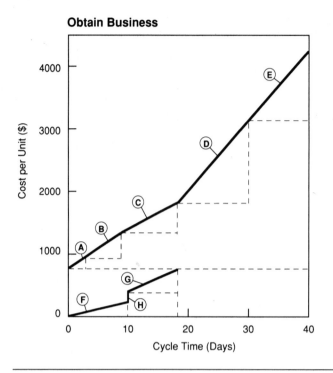

Figure 4-9
Micro Parallel Cost-Time Profile for business activities occurring in parallel.

to draw the Profile. Cost is shown as a dashed vertical line at the end of each activity cycle-time. Activity cycle-time is indicated by dashed lines. A sloped line (solid) connects back to the end of the previous activity's cycle time.

Finally, we analyze the profile. The reason for constructing the micro profile is to select areas of a business process for focused attention and improvement. Look for large elements of **cost** (figure 4-10); for large elements of **cycle time** (figure 4-11); and for indications of large areas of **operating cash** (figure 4-12).

These analyses will quickly pinpoint the parts of the process that have the largest potential for shrinking the profile. These areas deserve a closer look—a more detailed Cost-Time Profile and analysis—which is described next.

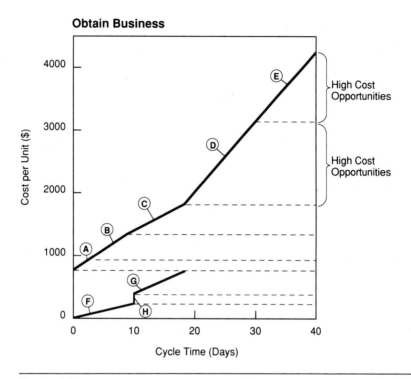

Figure 4-10
Micro Cost-Time Profile showing cost opportunity areas.

More Detailed Micro Cost-Time Profiles

Detailed micro Cost-Time Profiles are usually developed by teams of people assigned to address a specific opportunity for improvement. That opportunity has generally been identified in a macro Cost-Time Profile or in a higher-level micro Cost-Time Profile. The team then converts the detailed look into action plans. Improvement teams generally can develop detailed micro Cost-Time Profiles within an elapsed time of one to three weeks, working part-time.

The purpose of detailed Cost-Time Profiling is to identify critical areas for study, to expose and understand improvement opportunities, to generate ideas to address those opportunities, and to develop projects and implementation

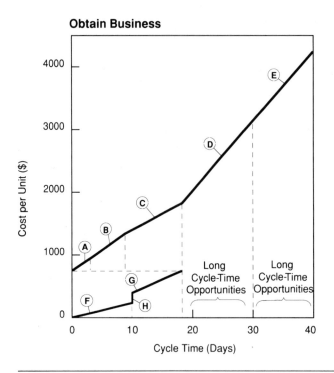

Obtain Business

Figure 4-11
Micro Cost-Time Profile showing cycle-time opportunity areas.

plans to meet improvement goals. During development, the micro profile team will generate some good ideas for shrinking an element of the profile. Record those ideas for future consideration, but continue developing the profile because the best ideas come when the entire area is well understood.

In the example that follows, we will develop a detailed look at the Process Order portion (Activity E) of the Obtain Business process (figure 4-5).

1. Construct the flow diagram.

It's usually a straightforward process to determine the current information flow or work flow by interviewing management and other people working in the area under study. Display the flow of work as a simple flow diagram like figure 4-13. At this level of analysis, each block will describe a single task rather than a complete activity.

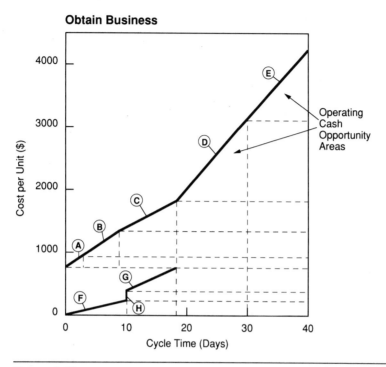

Figure 4-12
Micro Cost-Time Profile showing operating-cash opportunity areas.

One technique we've found very useful at Westinghouse is using removable adhesive Post-it Notes (or 3 × 5-inch index cards) to jot down the tasks and then to rearrange them until the proper sequence is achieved. Next, chart the flow of information and the corresponding work performed on the activity. Then validate the flow diagram by seeking and securing concurrence from the management and personnel involved in the activity.

Each block on the flow diagram should be assigned a task number for easy identification in the later steps.

2. Develop cost data.

Determine how many actual work hours (hands-on time) are expended in performing the task during the elapsed time period. Enter the actual work hours in the lower left-hand corner of each task block in the flow diagram (figure 4-14).

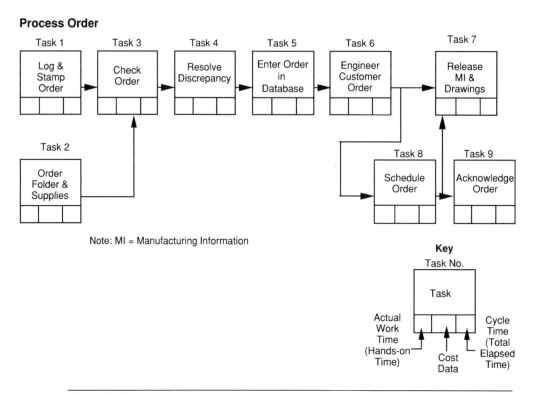

Figure 4-13
Flow diagram of the Process Order portion of the Obtain Business process.

Convert the cost for each task to dollars by multiplying actual work time by the average costing rate for the department or section performing the task. Accounting people should be able to provide the required costing rates. Place this dollar cost information in the lower center of each task block on the flow chart, as illustrated in figure 4-14. This area should also be used to record the cost of supplies or outside services and other expenses not included in the costing rate (shown in the Order Folder & Supplies block).

3. Prepare the Time-Cycle Chart.

Ask the people who perform the tasks specified on the flow chart to estimate the total elapsed time—the number of hours, days, or weeks between the time the work unit arrives at their work station (or leaves the prior work station) and

Process Order

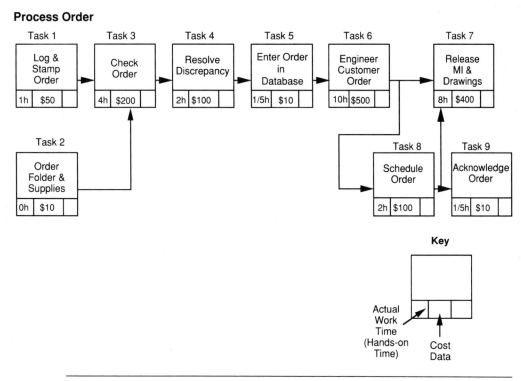

Figure 4-14
Flow diagram with actual-work-time values and cost data.

the time the completed work unit leaves their station. Approximate elapsed times are sufficient. Enter the average time for each task in the lower right-hand corner of each block with the appropriate unit of time (hours, days, weeks) as shown in figure 4-15.

Prepare a Time-Cycle Chart (figure 4-16) by plotting the elapsed times for each task along a time scale. The branches of the Time-Cycle Chart should mirror those of the flow diagram, except they will now be in time relationship as well as in work and information-flow relationship. To help identify each task, place the task number from the flow diagram below the line representing the cycle time of that task.

Returning to the people who supplied the time data, ask them to identify when each task's actual work hours are expended, along the elapsed time line.

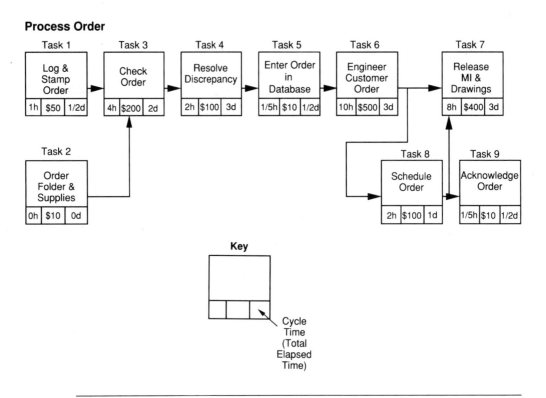

Figure 4-15
Completed flow diagram with cost and elapsed-time data.

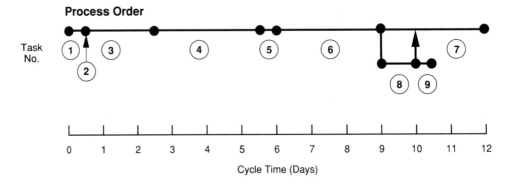

Figure 4-16
Time-Cycle Chart of the Process Order portion of the Obtain Business process.

Display the appropriate number of actual work hours (days, etc.) as small, drawn-to-scale rectangles or vertical lines at the points on the time cycle where they are worked. In figure 4-17, each vertical line represents one hour of working time.

Obtain the concurrence of the people involved with the process that the Time-Cycle Chart with actual hours is correct. Further validate the time data by reviewing the chart with the appropriate managers. Total elapsed times can also be checked against starts and completions reported on schedules. Actual work time can be validated by multiplying the number of work units processed in a month by the actual work time per unit, to determine whether the result approximates the time the person is expected to spend performing the task on a monthly basis.

The Cost-Time Profile can be constructed by plotting the number of hours worked directly on the vertical axis if time is the only cost element involved. However, when direct supplies cost is present—as in the Order Folder & Supplies task on the flow diagram in figure 4-13—the actual hours must be converted to dollars.

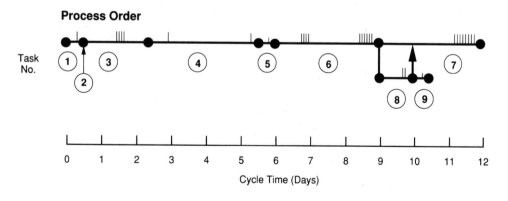

Figure 4-17
Time-Cycle Chart with actual hours. Each thin vertical line represents one hour in this example (shorter lines represent half an hour).

4. Construct the micro Cost-Time Profile.

Set up the Cost-Time Profile with the horizontal-axis scale (time) the same as the scale on the Time-Cycle Chart. The vertical-axis scale (cost) should equal the total cost of all the flow-diagram blocks. Figure 4-18 illustrates the result.

Start at the left end of the profile. Show the addition of cost and wait times for the first task on the Time-Cycle Chart. The addition of work (diagonal lines) occurs at the point in time indicated by the work-time rectangles or vertical lines on the Time-Cycle Chart. If the cost consists of supplies or outside services, it is shown as a vertical addition of cost at the specific time it is received (task 2 in figure 4-18).

The profile for the next task begins at the end of the previous task's profile. It will consist of horizontal wait periods, sloped work additions (whose height on the cost scale equals the cost of the task), vertical additions of supplies or outside services, or any combination of the three for each task on the Time-Cycle Chart.

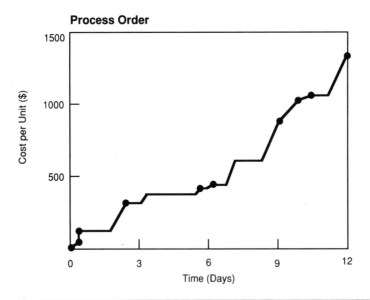

Figure 4-18
Detailed micro Cost-Time Profile.

Verify the Cost-Time Profile by assuring that the cost at the end of the last task, as read on the cost axis, equals the sum of the costs for all the tasks. Similarly, the time-axis length should be the same as the length of the Time-Cycle Chart.

With a detailed Cost-Time Profile in hand, an improvement team is ready to identify and understand opportunities and turn them into improvement actions.

How to Use the Micro Profile

A primary purpose of building a micro Cost-Time Profile is to develop improvement projects. This section discusses how to use the profiles to identify and understand opportunities for improvement, and then how to develop and evaluate ideas or solutions to achieve the improvement. Remember:

- Shrinking the cost axis will improve operating profit and reduce cash requirements.

- Shrinking the time axis will improve customer service, quality, and cash flow.

- Improving quality will improve cycle time, operating profit, customer service, cash flow, and operating cash.

Figure 4-19 illustrates the detailed Cost-Time Profile of the Process Order function (figure 4-18). Inspection shows three cycle-time opportunity areas (Resolve Discrepancy, Engineer Customer Order, and Prepare Manufacturing Information and Drawings) and two cost opportunity areas (Prepare Manufacturing Information and Drawings and Engineer Customer Order).

Quantifying these areas (figure 4-20) shows that the two high-cost areas account for 73% of the total cost as well as 50% of the cycle time. The one area of outside supplies—task 2 (figure 4-19)—is of relatively low cost and may not warrant further study at this time.

An excellent tool for understanding improvement opportunities and for generating improvement ideas is the **function diagram.** While a detailed description is beyond the scope of this book, a brief explanation will serve our purpose.

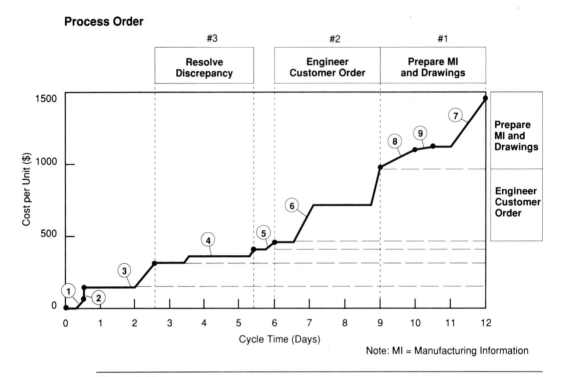

Figure 4-19
Identifying opportunities to improve the Process Order portion of the Obtain Business process. The names of the opportunity areas are shown in boxes above and to the right of the micro Cost-Time Profile.

Note that the function diagram is often referred to in value-analysis texts as a How-Why diagram.

We recommend constructing a function diagram of the entire process or sub-process—or, if the process is very large, diagramming at least the major sections where the opportunities are located.

Each function is stated in a verb-noun form. The team analyzes the tasks on a function diagram (figure 4-21 shows an example) by asking, "How is the task accomplished?" Each answer, stated as a verb-noun, is written on a Post-it Note. Functions generated by asking "How?" are arranged in logical relationship. The validity of each function can be checked by asking "Why is the function accom-

Process Order

Opportunity #	Cost		Time		Invisible Inventory	
	$	%	Days	%	Area $-Days	%
1. Week 9–12	510	37	3	25	3405	39
2. Week 6–9	500	36	3	25	1860	21
3. Week 2.5–5.5	100	7	3	25	930	11
•	•	•	•	•	•	•
•	•	•	•	•	•	•
•	•	•	•	•	•	•
Total	1380	100	12	100	8780	100

Figure 4-20
Quantifying opportunities for improving the Process Order function.

plished?"—and the function to the left should provide the answer. Developing this How-Why diagram aids greatly in clarifying complex information-based processes.

The function diagram also provides a creative tool—the team can begin at the right-hand side, with the sub-functions, and determine whether each one is necessary, or if it can be eliminated, reduced, combined, or performed in parallel. If the function is necessary, the team can prepare an alternative function diagram that explores "How else might the function be accomplished?" (figure 4-22). This function analysis can be continued until the team evolves new, more efficient and more effective ways to accomplish each necessary function.

The final steps are to quantify expected benefits, using the Cost-Time Profile; to prepare the details step-by-step to determine the cost of implementation; and to make recommendations to management.

Function Diagram

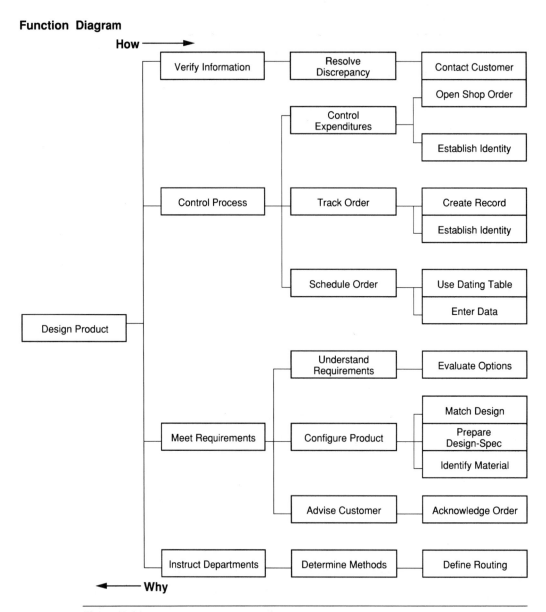

Figure 4-21
Function diagram for understanding profile opportunities.

Function Diagram

How else might we configure product?

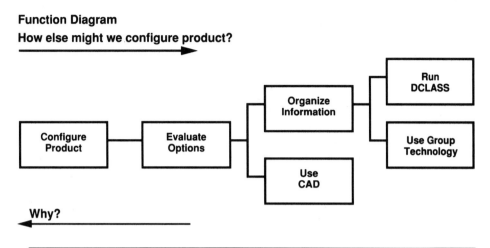

Figure 4-22
Function diagram used for generating ideas.

Using Cost-Time profiles in this way not only optimizes existing processes but also generates innovative ways to do the job in still less time, at lower cost.

Developing a Factory Micro Profile

The four-step process for constructing micro profiles, shown in figure 4-1, applies equally well to factory processes. To show this universality, this section details construction of a factory-oriented micro Cost-Time Profile for a function called Assemble Product. We'll use exactly the same procedure we followed in constructing the Obtain Business profile.

1. Construct the flow diagram.

Identify the major activities and their sequential relationships for the area being studied. Figure 4-23 diagrams the process flow for the Assemble Product function. Compare this diagram to figure 4-2 to see the similarity between this process's flow diagram and the one for the Obtain Business process.

Assemble Product

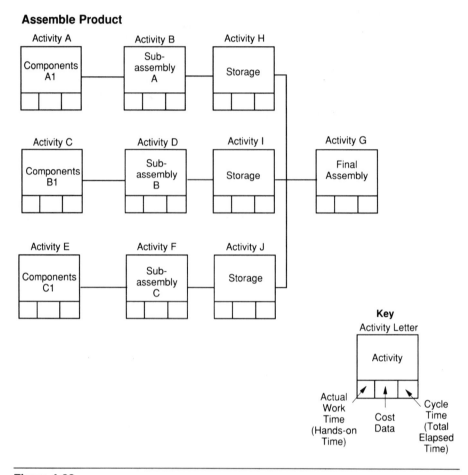

Figure 4-23
Micro flow diagram for the factory function Assemble Product.

Assemble Product

Ident. No.	Activity	Cost per Unit			
		Material	Labor	Overhead	Total Cost
1	Final Assembly	$32.25	$4.00	$6.00	$42.25
2	Sub-assembly A	3.25	2.00	2.50	7.75
3	Sub-assembly B	5.25	3.50	4.50	13.25
4	Sub-assembly C	2.25	4.00	5.00	11.25
5	Components A1	3.25	—	—	3.25
6	Components B1	5.25	—	—	5.25
7	Components C1	2.25	—	—	2.25

Figure 4-24
Cost-distribution form (data for flow diagram).

2. Develop cost data.

The material, labor, and overhead cost data per unit are shown in figure 4-24. This cost-distribution form compares with figure 4-3 for the Obtain Business function.

When the team is satisfied that the cost data are reasonably accurate, they enter these data into the cost block for each activity on the flow diagram, figure 4-25. Labor and overhead costs are combined for entry into the cost blocks for sub-assemblies and final assembly. This activity is performed the same as the Obtain Business step diagrammed in figure 4-4.

3. Prepare the Time-Cycle Chart.

First, determine the elapsed time for each activity. Enter these data in the lower right-hand block of each activity in the flow diagram, figure 4-26. The comparable diagram for the Obtain Business function is figure 4-5.

Assemble Product

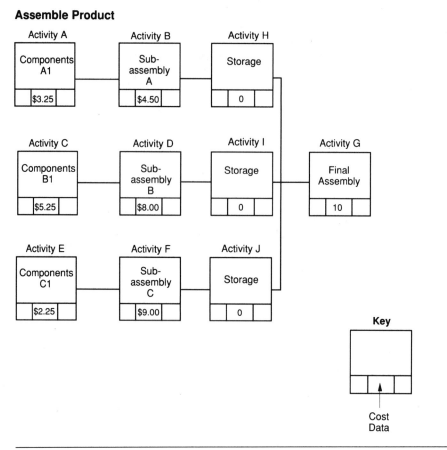

Figure 4-25
Micro flow diagram with cost data.

Assemble Product

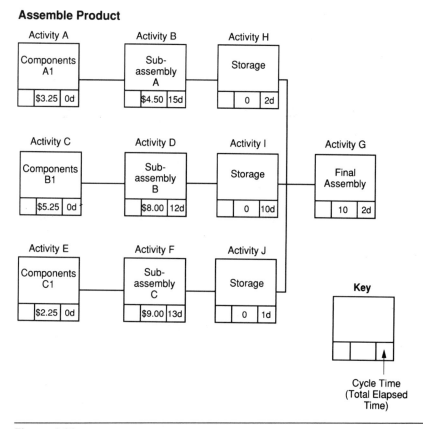

Figure 4-26
Micro flow diagram with cost and cycle-time data.

Next, prepare a Time-Cycle Chart (figure 4-27) by plotting the elapsed time for each activity along a time scale moving from right to left. This procedure will identify the critical path. It compares to figure 4-6 for the Obtain Business function.

4. Construct the Cost-Time Profile.

Using the cost and cycle-time data (figure 4-26) and the Time-Cycle Chart (figure 4-27), construct the factory Cost-Time Profile, figure 4-28. Follow the same procedure as was used to construct the Obtain Business Cost-Time Profile in figure 4-9.

Assemble Product

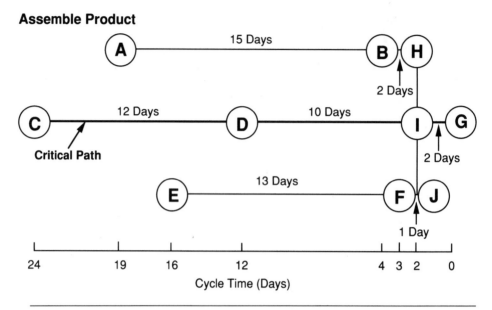

Figure 4-27
Time-Cycle Chart used in constructing micro Cost-Time Profile.

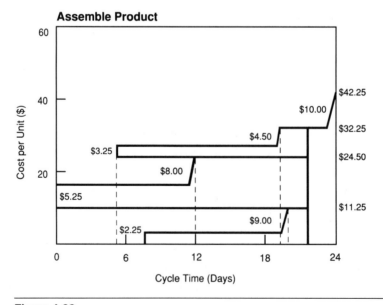

Figure 4-28
Factory Cost-Time Profile.

A Cost-Time
Guide to
Strategic Choices

This chapter is addressed primarily to CEOs and general managers, who must make strategic choices among numerous businesses and activities, all competing for scarce resources. In the strategic arena the Cost-Time perspective offers a new way of viewing such decisions as:

- How can we increase the shareholder value of the total business?
- Which activities should be expanded?
- Which activities should be considered as candidates for divestiture?
- How much cash is needed to run and grow a business?
- Which businesses should be financially acceptable acquisitions?
- What is the appropriate operating profit margin for a business?

The Cost-Time methodology does not replace traditional decision tools. It adds a new perspective to our decision-making processes, allowing us to view the business from the simultaneous perspectives of the income statement and the balance sheet. This new approach combines the focus of large corporations on

operating profit margins with the concentration of the small business owner on the **time cost of money.**

As described in chapter 2, we traditionally approach financial evaluation by examining the elements of the income statement (figure 5-1). This **cost perspective** aggregates the total cost of sales including factory costs and office costs (managed, strategic, committed, and so on). The difference between sales billed and the total cost of sales is operating profit, the bottom line.

In this cost-oriented view, two activities with identical income statements are regarded as equally viable financially. But in fact they are probably quite different. In particular, they will undoubtedly require different amounts of cash to operate and to grow—cash for inventory, for support activities in the office, and for receivables.

Elements of the Income Statement

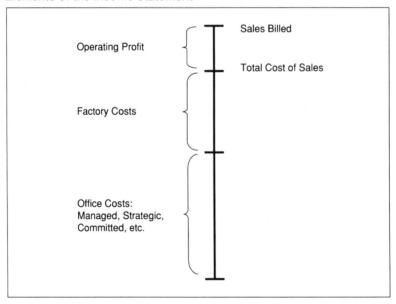

Figure 5-1
Typical cost-oriented financial perspective using only the income statement.

The macro Cost-Time Profile of a business (figure 5-2) adds the dimension of **time** to that of **cost.** In this Total Business Profile, the vertical axis retains the traditional income statement elements of cost, sales, and operating profit. The Cost-Time Profile adds a time dimension, so that the area under the profile is the dynamic-investment cash required to operate the business.

This point of view is generally not available to corporate executives, who have been trained to manage operating profit margins, selling price, and total cost. The Cost-Time Profile, accenting cash buildup over the months of a business cycle, redirects attention and opens new decision options for management. In a sense, it adds the entrepreneurial perspective of the small business owner who is focused on the amount of cash invested in the business and the time cost of that money.

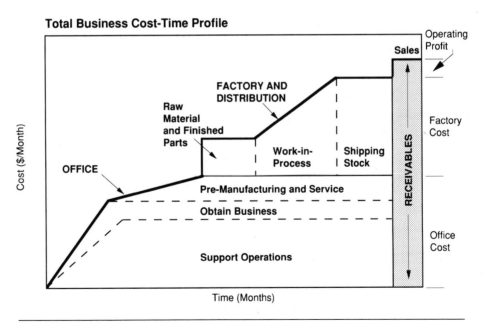

Figure 5-2
Macro Cost-Time Profile—adding the time dimension.

The Cash-Conversion Machine

In the Cost-Time perspective, we view the business as a process with inputs and outputs. The **input** to the business is **shareholder cash.** When we operate the business process, the output is **operating profit.** The Cash-Conversion model examines the efficiency of this input/output relationship.

In a way, we can look at the business as a machine for converting cash into margin! Figure 5-3 shows the idea, plotting profile cash (the area under the Total Business Cost-Time Profile, from the balance sheet but including the invisible inventory) as a percentage of sales against operating profit as a percentage of sales, from the income statement.

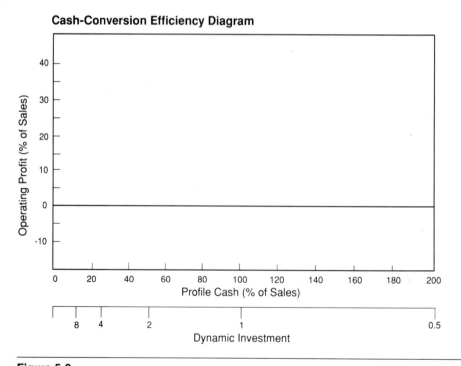

Figure 5-3
The Cash-Conversion Efficiency plane.

Notice that profile cash/sales is simply the inverse of the number of turns of the dynamic investment in the business (lower scale in figure 5-3), plotted on a logarithmic scale to convert it into a straight line.

If we plot our businesses on this field, what can we learn? Our strategic options depend heavily on where the business falls on the chart (figure 5-4). The numbers on the chart correspond with the numbers on the descriptions below. For example:

1. A business with low cash requirements (say, 20% of sales) and high margin (also 20% of sales, for example) has a cash-conversion efficiency of 1.0. A dollar of cash invested in the business to grow sales will return a dollar of operating profit margin (20 divided by 20).

2. On the other hand, a business which is a high-cash user (say, 200% of sales) may generate the same 20% operating profit on sales; but a dollar

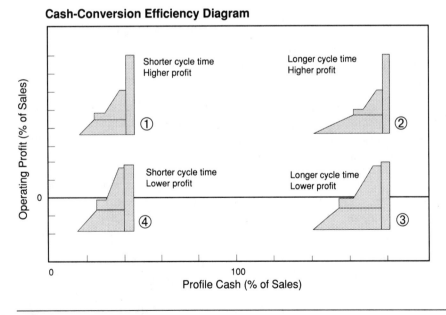

Cash-Conversion Efficiency Diagram

Figure 5-4
Comparison of operations (shown as Cost-Time Profiles) at different positions on the Cash-Conversion Efficiency plane.

invested to grow sales will return only 10 cents (20 divided by 200)! Cash-conversion efficiency is 0.1.

3. Even bigger problems lie ahead for the high-cash-using business (200% of sales) which generates relatively low margins, such as 2% of sales. Here, a dollar invested to grow sales will return only **one cent!** Cash-conversion efficiency here is only 0.01.

4. A fourth alternative is the low-cash user (20% of sales) which also generates low margins (2% of sales). In this case, an invested dollar to grow sales will return 10 cents. Notice that this example has the **same** cash-conversion efficiency (0.1) as example 2 above, despite a ten-to-one difference in operating profit percent of sales!

This last example illustrates the Performance Line shown in figure 5-5. All businesses falling on this line are essentially equal from the standpoint of financial performance. It is the relationship of output to input that matters—not the absolute value of the performance numbers. So, when we compare businesses using shareholder cash (from the balance sheet but including the invisible inventory) as well as operating profit (from the income statement), we may evaluate them quite differently than we would using the income statement alone.

This perspective suggests a simple criterion for business excellence: **A business creates value when it generates a return on shareholder cash which is much greater than the cost of equity.**

Management may pick the Performance Line slope that best matches its expectations, based on the shareholders' expected return for the risk associated with the investment of their cash. In effect, the Performance Line sets an objective for return on shareholder equity, including the "invisible inventory," and every business whose performance falls on that line is equally valuable to the enterprise.

Figure 5-5 illustrates this point using two Westinghouse divisions analyzed by the Productivity and Quality Center. Division A returns an operating profit of

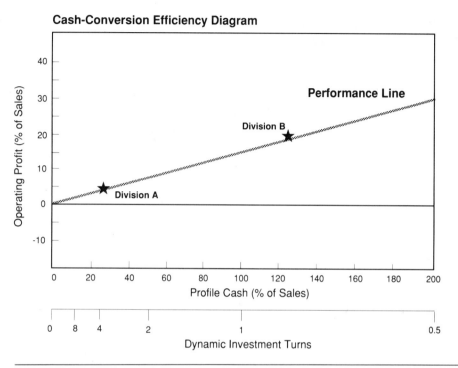

Figure 5-5
Stars show two different business operations with equivalent performance characteristics.

3.5% of sales—a puny effort by traditional standards. Division B, on the other hand, is something of a star, returning operating profit of 18% of sales.

Profile cash investment provides the other part of the story. Division A has a dynamic investment equal to only 25% of sales (four turns a year) compared to Division B, at a dynamic investment of 126% of sales (less than one turn). Division A, with its much greater turns, has a significantly shorter cycle time and smaller Cost-Time Profile than Division B.

Both divisions lie near the Performance Line, which marks 15% return on profile cash. From a financial and operating viewpoint, they are essentially equal performers. But they face different challenges and very different opportunities for improvement.

How to Succeed in the Cost-Time Value Game

As shown in figure 5-6, the desirable direction for improvement is **north-west**—reducing profile cash by shortening cycle times and increasing operating profit. This moves the business to a higher Performance Line, thus generating higher return on capital and increasing shareholder value. In a corporate environment, the released cash can be used to improve the business or acquire a new business, or it can be banked.

The cash-conversion efficiency view of the business provides an important yardstick for evaluating business strategies and actions. From a Cost-Time

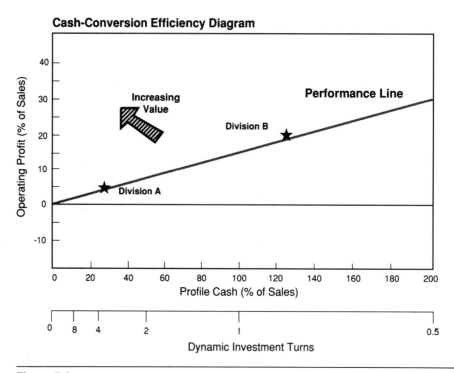

Figure 5-6
Increasing value performance moves an operation northwest, reducing profile cash, increasing turns, and increasing operating profit relative to sales.

perspective, activities are "good" if they in fact move the operating unit in a northwesterly direction.

How can this Cost-Time perspective aid a general manager in making strategic decisions that will lead to a more successful future for the business?

The following example describes an actual Westinghouse business unit—with annual billings of some $950 million—analyzed by the Westinghouse Productivity and Quality Center. We'll follow the analysis and itemize the decisions and their consequences, as the improvement team went through the Cost-Time process in strategic planning for the unit. We'll call it the Power Sequencer Business Unit.

The unit designs, manufactures, and sells engineered components and assemblies for power sequencing. Its principal customers are electric utilities and large electrical contractors. The business unit has six operating divisions, and includes 31 plants in the U.S. and overseas.

The analysis begins by constructing macro Cost-Time Profiles for each of the plants in each division (figure 5-7 shows one division and its five plants). Each plant essentially represents an individual product line. The total division profile is obtained by summing the profiles of the plants.

At this level of detail, some improvement opportunities—in the areas of cost, cycle time, and cash—are already clear. Figure 5-8 compares the six divisions, using the same scales for cost and time axes in all six Cost-Time Profiles. Obviously, there is a wide diversity in both cycle times and costs among these six operating divisions. From an overall management perspective, the opportunities are becoming clearer.

Summing the division profiles provides a Total Business Unit Cost-Time Profile for the entire Power Sequencer Business Unit (figure 5-9). These data show the unit's profile cash is 52% of sales (approximately two dynamic investment turns per year) and operating profit is 4.8% of sales—modest and improvable.

An interesting discovery at this point is the magnitude of cash required to run support and office activities: invisible inventory for the unit is $262 million or 53% of the total cash. Factory inventory is $130 million (26% of the total), and

Profile Comparison

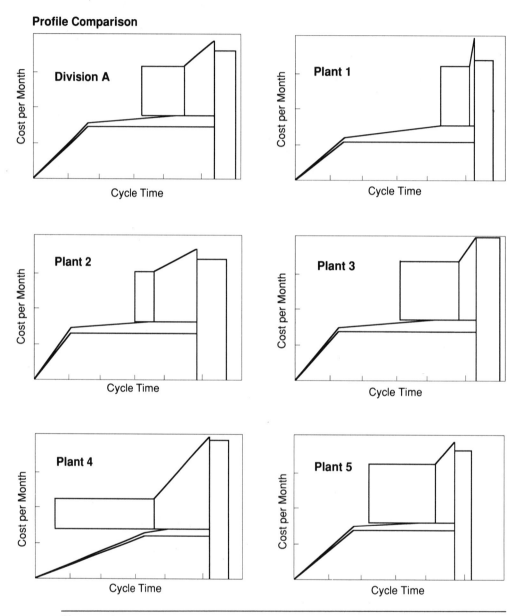

Figure 5-7
Macro Cost-Time Profiles of a division and its five plants.

Profile Comparison

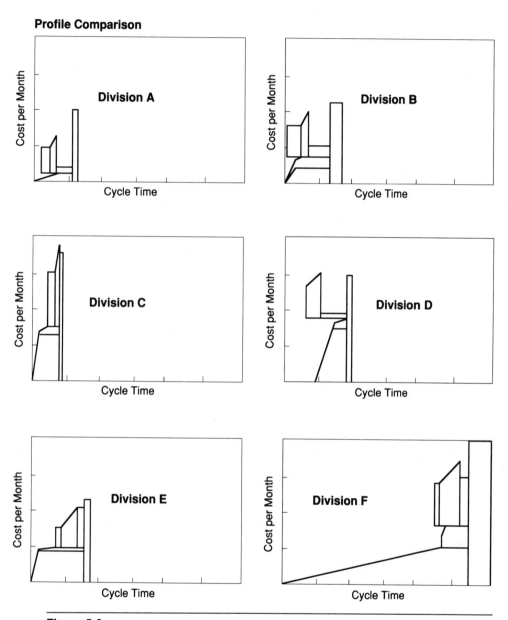

Figure 5-8
Macro Cost-Time Profiles of the six divisions in the business unit, drawn to the same scale.

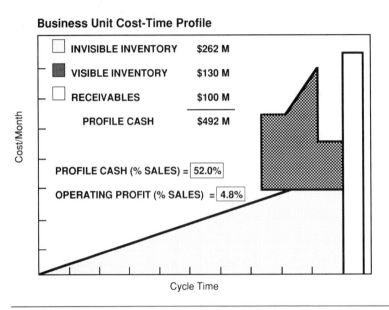

Figure 5-9
Macro Cost-Time Profile for a business unit.

receivables, at $100 million, account for 21% of the cash. This proportion—heavily weighted toward white-collar operations—is a typical pattern. Our greatest improvement opportunities are often found in the office.

One immediate and obvious conclusion is that, for each incremental dollar of sales, this business will need to invest 52 cents: 14 cents in inventory, 10 cents in receivables, and 28 cents in white-collar and support operations—unless significant changes are made in the way the business operates. Decisions about those changes are important strategic considerations.

The next step in strategic decision making is to rank the divisions and plants. To do this, we use the Cash-Conversion Efficiency Diagram (figure 5-10).

The business unit is plotted as a centroid (black square) at 52% profile cash/sales and 4.8% operating profit/sales. Divisions are plotted in the same fashion and indicated by stars in figure 5-10; the plants are plotted as circles with diameters proportional to sales volume. From this diagram, we can begin to make strategic judgments. For some businesses, the team would plot each

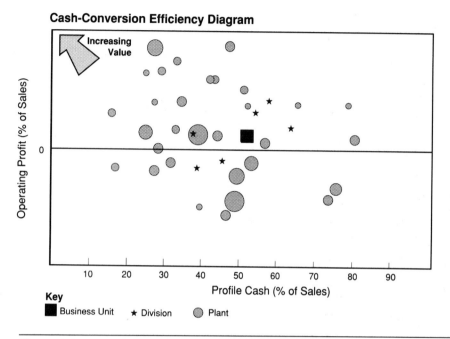

Figure 5-10
Business Unit, division, and plant cash-conversion efficiency.

product line as a circle on the cash-conversion field; in this case, the team chose to plot plants because each plant is essentially devoted to a single product family.

To begin working with this diagram, draw horizontal and vertical lines through the business-unit centroid (figure 5-11). This segments the field into four quadrants, which we have named the Value-Enhancement quadrant, High-Time quadrant, Black-Hole quadrant, and High-Cost quadrant. The most desirable operations are obviously in the upper left, in the Value-Enhancement quadrant. This is the most viable area for a business to be—the area where continuing the Total Quality improvement process will continue to build value for the enterprise.

Of course, there are other elements that strategic planners must consider. We are taking primarily a financial and operational look at the business. Planners must also keep in mind the political, public-opinion, customer, and marketing

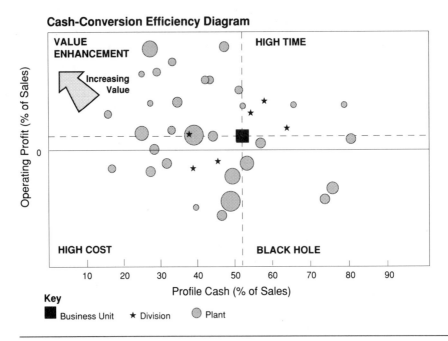

Figure 5-11
Analyzing operations on the cash-conversion efficiency plane.

factors that can affect the stability and viability of the business. Operationally, though, the Value-Enhancement quadrant is the success field.

What about activities falling in the Black Hole? They are either newborn businesses, necessary for growth, or sick businesses that detract in margin and turnover and could well be candidates for divestiture or closure. The important question is: how can these operations justify their continued existence? If they cannot, they should be removed.

The operations with high cycle times or high cost require prompt attention to try moving them to the Value-Enhancement quadrant.

To further quantify the issues from the Cost-Time perspective, we must add the Performance Line, which defines excellent performance from the point of view of a particular business (figure 5-12). In the Power Sequencer Business Unit, the team proposed a line that defined an 18% return on dynamic investment.

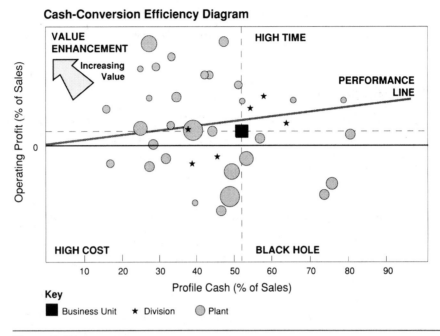

Figure 5-12
Selecting the Performance Line for all business operations.

This line establishes excellence for each operation, assuming that all businesses have equal risk to the shareholders (a safe assumption in this case).

If the business unit elects to maintain its present cycle times—leading to the current profile cash position of 52% of sales—the unit as a whole will require an operating profit of 9.5% of sales to reach the line of excellence. By reducing cycle time and profile cash, the unit can attain excellence at lower levels of operating profit/sales. There are clearly many alternatives available; at this point of the analysis, the issues are visible and clear, and objectives can be quantified.

Examining Strategic Options

Figure 5-12 also allows the management team to address some key strategic questions (assuming that the operating units, excluding new businesses, have remained in their respective quadrants for a statistically meaningful period of time). Several key questions can be addressed by examining a cash-conversion field.

Which businesses should be grown?

Residents of the Value-Enhancement quadrant are prime candidates for growth investments. They are the leaders in operating profit margins and cash turnover, and their growth is most likely to drive the business unit in the direction of increasing value.

Which businesses should be considered candidates for divestiture?

Residents of the Black-Hole quadrant, except newborn businesses, are the primary choices. They are detractors in both operating profit margin and cash turnover. However, caution is indicated: our experience has shown that some operating units may be in the Black Hole due to factors outside their control. For example, the business unit may be allocating them an unreasonable overhead or may be forcing them to buy components from a sister plant—possibly one in the Value-Enhancement quadrant—at prices above market levels.

How much cash is needed to run and grow a business?

If the business will continue to operate unchanged, and costs are permitted to grow linearly—as is all too often the case in growth situations—then the profile cash/sales axis provides a direct answer. A business with a profile cash/sales coordinate of 80 has consumed 80 cents in dynamic investment for every dollar of sales it is generating. Further, it will demand the same level of consumption for every dollar of incremental sales it generates in the future. Contrast this performance with that of a business having a coordinate of 20, and the impact of cash turnover is evident.

What businesses would be financially acceptable acquisitions?

Any operation eventually capable of driving the business unit in a northwesterly direction would, financially, be an acceptable acquisition. The immediate effect of an acquisition will be to drive the business unit eastward, due to the cash investment. The critical element is the subsequent near-term forecasted movement of the acquired operation.

What target should be set for operating profit margin?

> The Performance Line set by the business unit manager is where every operating unit should be, at a minimum. The management challenge is to move the units that are below the Performance Line. Movement can be northward (margin improvement), westward (turnover improvement), or any combination that lands the business on or above the Performance Line.
>
> The planning team can now summarize business unit opportunities on a matrix (figure 5-13), and they can calculate financial consequences of each alternative. This kind of discussion leads to consideration of a variety of options, opportunities, and alternative scenarios.

Putting It All Together:
A Baldrige-Winning Performance

> The Cost-Time perspective, in its fullest application, is used to select specific improvement projects and to quantify their effects on operating profit and cash turns. By using micro and macro Cost-Time Profiles, as well as Cash-

Business-Unit Improvement Opportunities

Operating Unit	COST			TIME	CASH			VALUE			
	Support/ Sales	Office/ Sales	Factory/ Sales	Pur Order Release to Ship	Inventory/ Sales	Receiv/ Sales	Invisible/ Sales	Divest	Transfer	Sub-contract	Shrink Profile
A											
B											
C											
D											
etc.											

Figure 5-13
Matrix used to plot business-unit improvement opportunities for strategic planning.

Conversion Efficiency Analysis, a management team can measure, evaluate, rank, and select options to attain its goals.

Here's how one Westinghouse division did it, using the Cost-Time methodology as an integral part of their Total Quality planning. The Westinghouse Commercial Nuclear Fuel Division (CNFD), 1988 winner of the Malcolm Baldrige National Quality Award, used the Cost-Time technique as their primary management tool for business improvement from 1983 onward. Here, published for the first time, is their story.

The basic Westinghouse Cost-Time Operational Value-Creation Process is shown conceptually in figure 5-14.

- The Macro Planning phase involves the division general manager and staff in addressing three key questions:

  - **Where are we now?** The macro Cost-Time Profile (chapter 3) provides the answer.

  - **Where do we want to go?** This answer requires goal setting.

  - **How do we plan to get there?** The Opportunities Workshop addresses this question.

  The impact of planned actions is monitored on the cash-conversion efficiency plane.

- In the Develop Quantified Solutions phase, process-improvement teams convert the outputs of the Opportunities Workshop into quantified improvement projects, using a variety of methodologies including the micro Cost-Time Profiles described in chapter 4.

- Finally, in the Implementation phase, the teams initiate the projects, implement and measure the results.

This Operational Value-Creation Process was adopted by the Commercial Nuclear Fuel Division of Westinghouse for the purpose of making radical improvement. By 1987, after three years of steady growth, the division management observed that market forces were likely to adversely impact their operating profit margins. By 1990, they reckoned, the situation would be deteriorating, as shown in figure 5-15.

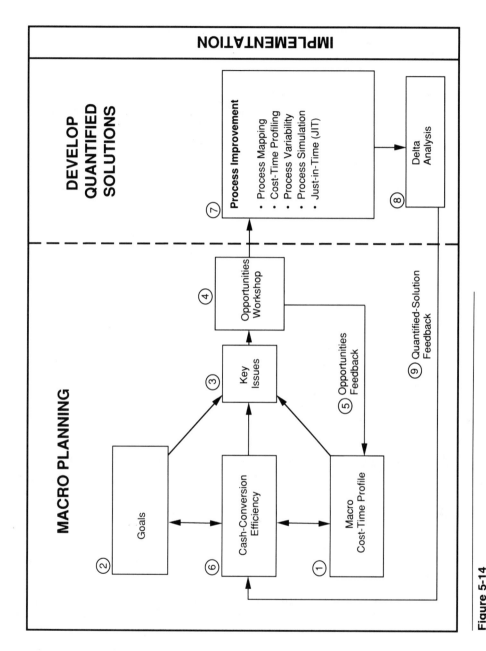

Figure 5-14

The value-enhancement process in use at Westinghouse.

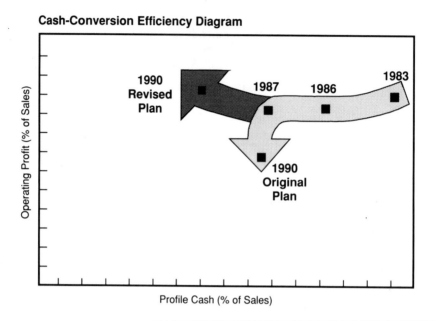

Figure 5-15
Effects of Cost-Time Analysis on 1990 planning targets at the Westinghouse Commercial Nuclear Fuel Division.

The general manager was unwilling to accept this situation, even though the forecasted 1990 operating profit margin would still have been outstanding by corporate standards. Instead, the general manager set as a 1990 objective the revised plan shown in figure 5-15.

The issue was, clearly, how to get there.

The first step was to construct a forecasted 1990 macro Cost-Time Profile (figure 5-16), showing the anticipated operation in 1990 if present operations were simply extended for three years.

Then the general manager and staff conducted a two-day Opportunities Workshop, examining some 60 value-enhancement opportunities aimed at shrinking the Cost-Time Profile relative to sales. They then distilled the 60 opportunities

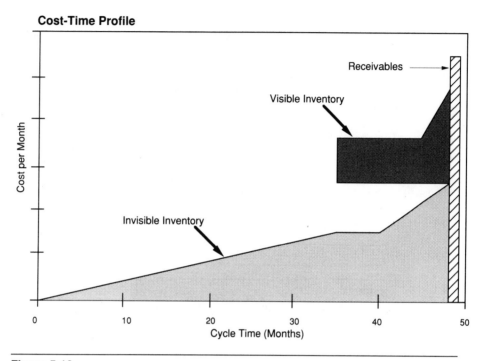

Figure 5-16
The original forecasted 1990 Cost-Time Profile from the Commercial Nuclear Fuel Division's strategic plan.

into 12 potential projects (figure 5-17). They analyzed and quantified each project for its impact on cost and cycle time, then displayed it in stand-alone fashion on a cash-conversion efficiency plane (figure 5-18). The numbers refer to the projects listed in figure 5-17, each plotted without reference to any other project. The shaded square (lower right) represents the forecasted position of the division if nothing changed.

Figure 5-19 shows the cumulative impact of all 12 projects. At this point, the team knew that the general manager's 1990 goal was attainable.

Figure 5-20 shows both the 1990 profile originally forecasted and the projected shrunken 1990 profile which assumed that all 12 projects were successfully

Twelve Projects for Improvement

Opportunity Number	Impact Type	Improvement-Project Description
2	Cost	Improve product efficiency
6	Cost	Reduce assessments, G&A, and other fixed costs
7	Price	Achieve price increase
8	Volume	Increase manufacturing volume
14	Cost	Reduce DM & PFE costs
17	Time	Reduce engineering development cycle time
18	Time	Reduce pre-manufacturing engineering cycle time
19	Price	Reduce raw material holding time
21	Time	Reduce manufacturing cycle time
26	Cost	Reduce finished parts costs
29	Cost	Reduce engineering costs
54	Volume	Increase engineering service and technology transfer sales

Figure 5-17
Value-enhancement opportunities at the Commercial Nuclear Fuel Division.

implemented. Now the division management team had a clear, quantitative road-map for achieving their three-year strategic-plan goals—and they had a direct linkage between individual improvement projects and overall financial goals.

Commented general manager Mead D'Amore: "The Operational Value-Creation Process did five things for us:

- It set a strategic direction for excellence.

- It quantified and prioritized the right things to do to create more share-holder value.

- It provided a bridge from the strategic plan to the operating plan.

- It provided a tool to measure ongoing progress.

- It mobilized our organization to continue its world-class "Total Quality journey."

For the record, the Commercial Nuclear Fuel Division exceeded its 1990 revised plan objectives, using Cost-Time Profiles to improve performance.

Cash-Conversion Efficiency Diagram

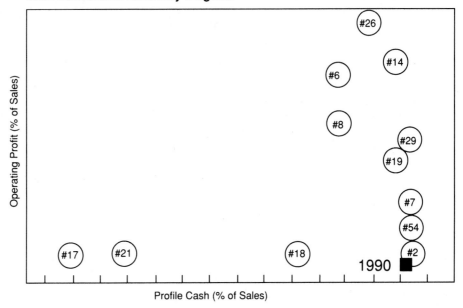

Figure 5-18
Impact of individual improvement projects on cash and operating profit. The numbers refer to the projects listed in figure 5-17; the shaded square represents the original forecasted position of the division with no improvement projects implemented.

Cash-Conversion Efficiency Diagram

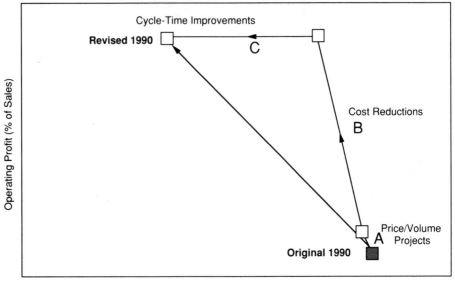

Profile Cash (% of Sales)

Figure 5-19
Cash-conversion efficiency impact of selected improvement projects, ignoring the effects of cycle-time improvements on costs.

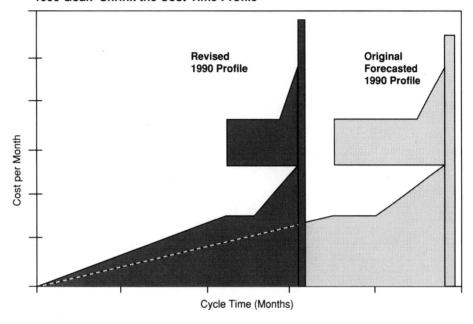

Figure 5-20

Effects of Cost-Time Analysis on projected operations improvement. (The area under the dashed white line is part of the original forecasted profile.)

Appendix A.
The "K Factor"

(Note: Most of this material was developed by the Westinghouse Headquarters Manufacturing Department during the 1960s and early seventies. This appendix is drawn primarily from material published by that group in October 1974.)

In constructing Cost-Time Profiles of factory work-in-process (WIP) inventory, Westinghouse people found a convenient way to convert months' supply data (or days' supply, weeks' supply, etc.) into average cycle times in the factory. This calculation involves a dimensionless profile factor which we have termed the "K Factor."

"K" describes the portion of the cycle/material value rectangle during which material is part of work-in-process. The formula for work-in-process inventory is:

$$WIP(m) = K \times C \times R$$

where $WIP(m)$ = value of work-in-process material for a given profile in which:

K = Profile factor derived from the inventory picture

C = Cycle (number of periods)

R = Rate of flow (inventory dollars per period)

When looking at work-in-process inventory, the rate-of-flow (R) value is the inventory output per period from work-in-process and is normally flowing on to the shipping department for direct shipment to customers or to components or finished-products storerooms.

The rate of flow to be used is the average rate of flow for the production level to be supported, using either current or forecasted data. The intent is for the calculated inventory standard to reflect the business level or production level planned. The minor variances in production rates from month to month should be averaged out. Major trend changes due to increases or decreases in business deserve a separate calculation for each new rate of flow.

Cycle (C) is the manufacturing cycle time required to produce the components and/or finished products being studied. Manufacturing cycle time starts with the first material charges to the shop order or customer order and finishes with the completed order moving out of work-in-process.

The time periods for cycle definition can be months, weeks, or days. Regardless of the time period used, make sure the rate of flow (inventory dollars per period) is expressed in comparable terms.

Figure A-1 shows a product with a four-month manufacturing cycle. In this example, 100% of the material is in final assembly and test for the last month (right side of picture). At the left, in the first two months, 25% of the inventory cost was raw material being machined and fabricated into components. At the beginning of the third month, components amounting to 25% of the inventory cost for the product were released to sub-assembly. At the beginning of the fourth month, additional parts and sub-assemblies amounting to 50% of the inventory cost were added to final assembly.

After drawing the inventory picture, we determine the K Factor by counting the blocks (8) under the profile line and dividing the count by the total number of blocks (16) in the field. Therefore, this picture has a K Factor of 0.50 (8 blocks divided by 16 blocks).

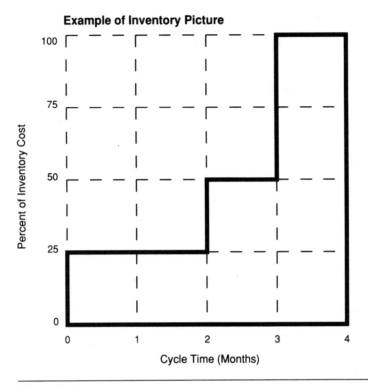

Figure A-1
Inventory example where K = 0.50.

In many factory processes, especially those using just-in-time principles, the work-in-process (materials) buildup is virtually continuous, and the process is diagrammed as a diagonal straight line. To calculate the K Factor when cost buildup can be approximated by a straight line (figure A-2), the formula is:

$$K = \frac{A + B}{2B}$$

where:

A = Cost buildup (in $) at the beginning of the work-in-process cycle (basically raw material cost)

and

B = Cost buildup (in $) at the end of the work-in-process cycle

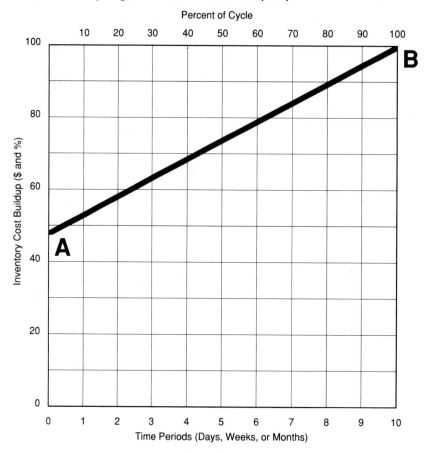

Inventory Worksheet

Inventory Segment: Work-in-Process (WIP)

Figure A-2
Straight-line inventory buildup worksheet.

Using the K Factor in the cycle-time equation allows us to convert months' supply data into average cycle-time calculations, with the formula:

$$\text{Cycle time} = \frac{\text{Months' supply}}{K}$$

Note that for storeroom-type inventories (raw materials, finished parts, and shipping stock), $K = 1$, because $A = B$.

Appendix B.
Aging Chart Analysis

Among the outputs of the macro-profile diagnostic analysis is a list of opportunities aimed at reducing cycle times and reducing the cost of portions of business processes. In the case of factory inventories, a word of caution is sometimes important: these investments may contain surplus, inactive, or obsolete items that can dramatically shrink the base available for rapid cycle-time reductions.

To clarify this situation, we use an Aging Chart Analysis. As a simple example, we can construct aging charts for raw material, finished parts, work-in-process, and shipping stocks associated with the inventory being studied:

Table B-1
Aging Chart for Factory Inventory

| | CURRENT MONTH ($000) | |
	Actual	**Months' supply**
Raw material	3200	3.2
Finished parts	2770	4.1
Shipping stocks	4920	4.3

The data and information required to construct aging charts should be readily available from the controller's office. Figures B-1, B-2, and B-3 illustrate possible aging charts for raw material, finished parts, and shipping stock. Dollar values, months' supply, and number of items are shown for each segment.

In figure B-1, for example, raw material has 147 items in the range of 0–3 months' supply, with a cumulative dollar value of $880,000. In the range of 3–12 months' supply, there are 184 items with a total value of $2 million. For greater than 12 months' supply, there are 370 items with a cumulative value of $320,000.

Analysis of these three aging charts indicates where traditional just-in-time methods would have little improvement impact—such as in figure B-2 where the $1.85 million of finished-parts inventory is in the range of greater than 12

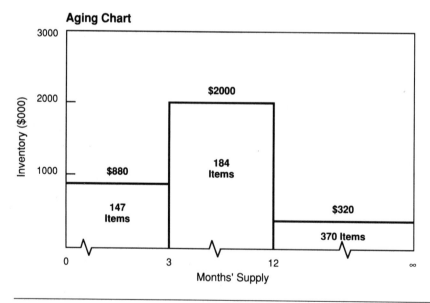

Figure B-1
Aging chart for raw material.

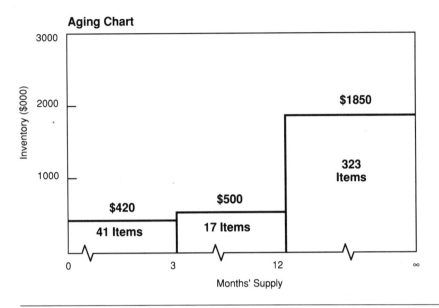

Figure B-2
Aging chart for finished parts.

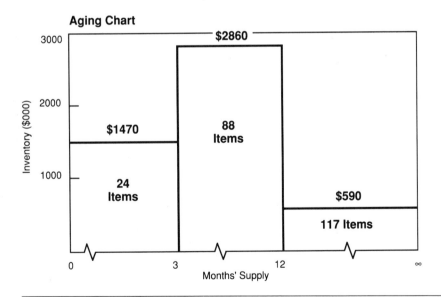

Figure B-3
Aging Chart for shipping stock.

months' supply. In this case, scrapping or a "fire sale" may be the only solution—with possibly unacceptable effect on operating profit.

This use of Aging Chart Analysis provides a way to delve deeper into the area of inventory assessment, to discover specific means of shrinking the profile.

INDEX